Memories

of

Chelmsford

*The publishers would like to thank the following companies for their
support in the production of this book*

Main Sponsor
High Chelmer Shopping Centre

APU

Bolingbroke & Wenley

James Budgett Sugars Limited

Edmund Carr

Chelmsford Star Co-operative Society

Frederick J French Limited

M Lucking & Sons

Marconi Applied Technologies

The M&G Group

Miami Hotel

New Hall School - The Priory of the Resurrection

Ridley's Brewery

First published in Great Britain by True North Books Limited
England HX5 9AE

Copyright © True North Books Limited, 2000

ISBN 1 903204 29 1

*Text, design and origination by True North Books Limited
Printed and bound in Great Britain*

Memories

of

Chelmsford

Contents

Introduction

Bring out the photographs in any company, and, provided that they contain scenes or people who have touched the lives of each, memories and recollections will be sparked. Each memory igniting another - the school, a mutual friend, a place, an event. Memories flood out. There is nothing quite like an old photograph to make us laugh at the styles we wore and to make us wonder at the speed time has slipped by. There is a regret that time might have been better spent, but it is bitter sweet. 'If only'.

Time is a softener of experience; we forget the diphtheria, scarlet fever, and various childhood illnesses and all the many discomforts of the past. The cod liver oil flavour is quickly overcome by the orange juice which followed as we were given much needed vitamins during the war years. The labels attached to the children who were evacuated. The tears of many partings. Thankfully, the memories which endure tend to be the joys of homecomings, times with friends at the local dance hall, or meeting a friend at the picture house. Suddenly we have a craving for reunions.

We forget the cold mornings in a house without the benefit of central heating. Getting dressed, or sometimes getting bathed, in front of the fire. Learning the now forgotten skills of rolling newspaper to light the coal or coke. Laying a knitting needle diagonally across the page and rolling it to make a tube, then folding it into a knot. It was the last job at night, except for filling the hot-water bottles and turning off the lights.

Continued overleaf

This picture of High Street featuring the Saracens Head Hotel in the foreground was taken around 1968

From previous page: Placing a newspaper across the fire opening, in the dangerous way that Granny did, would make the draft blow the flames white hot. We don't often remember that it was our job to shovel the coal into a bucket and carry it up the cellar steps. It was fun watching the coal-man tip the sacks of coal down the hole in the pavement outside directly into the cellar. 'Make sure you count them', mother would instruct us. And how she would grumble if there were any stones mixed with the coal, or if the sacks contained too much dust instead of shiny black lumps of coal. We would laugh at the way the coalman would wear a coal sack, opened down one side, over his head and covering his back and neck. He did it to protect his body from the lumpy sacks that he rocked onto his shoulders from the flat-backed lorry. We forget, until reminded by our treasured photographs, that the smoke issued from every chimney in the street as well as from the factories. Words, like 'smog', had to be added to our vocabularies to describe the pea-soup mixture of smoke and fog that regularly blanketed us.

The 'hand-me-downs', from older members of the family, in the 'make do and mend' years of the war. Some were lucky enough to the middle boy, in a family of three, with an older sister, but the younger brother always complained bitterly. We smile now in retrospect, at the skilful way

that the ladies made underwear from parachute silk, and clothes modified from older garments to appear more fashionable. Little wonder that schools taught such crafts as knitting, sewing and embroidery. Dads became the family cobbler, and many a last is now painted as a decorative feature of the conservatory or garden. Objects too, it seems, acquire a different status with time.

Just as the schools adopted the architectural pattern of the church in their early days, many of them with a spire, so the television often resembled the radio until it developed its own personality. The motorcar was built on a chassis resembling the shafts of the horse drawn cart, with the engine slipped into the shanks

April 1963 when Her Majesty Queen Elizabeth and HRH Prince Philip visited the town for the age-old tradition of distributing the Royal Maundy Money.

HRH Princess Margaret's visit to the town on Tuesday 24 April 1973 in her role as Deputy Colonel in Chief of the Royal Anglian Regiment to open the Essex Regiment Museum in Oaklands Park

The junction of High Street and Springfield Road in a picture dating from the 1950s

where the horse had been tethered. They all seemed like logical developments, but now seem so amusing with the wisdom of hindsight.

Cities and towns develop and evolve in the same way, and photographs of them bring back those warm recollections. Chelmsford, like many other towns grew around a crossing place on a river. The Romans had a fort to the south of the river at Moulsham, which was given the honour of the title of Caesaromagus. Probably built as a post to guard the river crossings, but developed into a small market community called Caesaromagus - the market place of Caesar. When the Romans left, the fort and the large mansion, which had been built there, fell into disuse. It had never gained the importance of the settlement at Colchester or that at St Albans.

From the stone bridge Chelmsford's roads radiate. Soon it became a vital stopping point for the coaches travelling from London to Colchester and other towns in Essex and beyond. The Inns provided accommodation for the many passengers, the markets within

the town grew, and Chelmsford developed. Charles Dickens is reputed to have stayed at the Old Black Boy Inn in Springfield Road, as he travelled to and from London with news of the cases tried at Ipswich. In his book, 'Pickwick' the Inn is mentioned.

The major industries, which have been welcomed and valued in the town, have ensured its prosperity and carried the people through times of depression in other parts of the country. During the war years Chelmsford paid dearly. It was a target for enemy planes because of its industries. But now the city's contribution to the war effort can be looked back on with justifiable pride.

The High Street contained many grand houses, whose purpose changed over time, but we can still see evidence of them if we raise our eyes when walking down that busy street. These changes will be gently remembered by those who browse over these valuable records of the town's proud history; they will have some pangs of regret, but will also know that the progress is inevitable.

Street scenes

Memories of CHELMSFORD

Shops such as Boots the Chemist, the Maypole Dairy and the Fifty Shilling Tailor were part of life around 1930, when this photograph was taken. FST, as the latter was known for short, really did sell suits for fifty bob (£2.50 in decimal currency), and they also prided themselves on their tradition of using all-British labour. The Maypole Dairy used to have mouthwatering window displays of dairy produce and groceries, in the days before so many items came prepacked. In the far distance we can see the Marconi masts reaching up into the sky. The Marconi works, which provided the sound transmitter for the capital's new TV station at Crystal Palace, represented the cutting edge of technology at the time. Younger readers born into the computer age might not be impressed by the two decades plus which elapsed between Marconi's pioneering wireless transmissions in the 1890s and the beginning of BBC radio broadcasting in 1922, but the impact of radio on daily life was immense. Listening to the wireless was a novel recreation, but it was also a major leap forward into mass communication, and its importance during the second world war cannot be overestimated. Regular television broadcasts began in 1936, but very few households had a TV set. Instead, most people watched images of the war and other news items on the newsreels shown at cinemas between the films.

Essex Libraries

Essex Libraries

Above: Where were you at 11.45 AM on the 20th October 1951? If you were riding on a motor cycle along High Street you may well be the person featured dead centre in this photograph. On this day at least it was possible to travel by bike without getting wet through or frozen to death; the shadows tell their own tale: this was a fine autumn day with the sun shining brightly. On the left of the picture are two cars painted black; it was possible to get cars in other colours - at a price - but until the 1960s Henry Ford's dictum that 'you can have any colour you want as long as it's black' seemed to satisfy most folk. Certainly in the pre-smokeless fuel days few drivers would have been happy to own a white car! The row of buildings on the left hand side of the scene houses WG

Essex Libraries

Webber, gents hairdressers, whilst further along can be seen the Queens Hotel and Baxter's butchers. What is perhaps most surprising to modern eyes is how little traffic appears in the picture at just fifteen minutes before noon. The Belisha beacons on their black and white painted poles seem quite superfluous: certainly there was as yet no need for a pelican crossing with traffic lights to actually stop vehicles for the benefit of pedestrians.

Above right: Road works were ahead of drivers on the day this late 1950s scene was captured, and warning signs suggest to motorists that they might have to take an alternative route to wherever they want to go. So what's new? This 'Alice through the Looking Glass' approach to motoring (head off in the opposite direction to your destination) has become familiar to drivers around most towns and cities, who find themselves facing holes in the road

and sets of temporary traffic lights with tedious regularity. Moulsham Street was characterised by countless independent retailers who ran their small but successful businesses along this normally busy road. Doubtless they would have had something to say about the disruption caused to their livelihoods when the workmen paid this visit! The 1950s saw many changes in Britain's shopping habits. In 1954 all rationing in Britain was ended, bringing to an end the last of wartime belt tightening restrictions. Brand names once more appeared on certain food products, and young people were amazed to realise that products such as margarine could be labelled as Stork or Summer County instead of just being plain old foul tasting margarine. The end of the decade saw the rise of the self service store. The trend started slowly, but it was relentless and spelled the end for many of the independent retailers in Chelmsford and elsewhere.

Below: No one can live in, or visit, Chelmsford without the name of Judge Tindal becoming familiar to them. There is a square named after him and a statue in that square erected in his honour. The inscription reads, 'Erected A D 1850. To preserve for all time the image of a Judge, whose administration of English Law - directed by serene wisdom - animated by the purest love of justice - endeared by unwearied kindness and graced by the most lucid style will be held by his country in undying remembrance'. The bronze statue stands on the site where the Conduit once stood when the square was also named Conduit Square. The Conduit was moved to a position at the junction of High Street and Springfield Road.

Born at this house in Moulsham Street, he went on in life to become a man of great stature deserving of the above recognition. His name, and those of three other influential men, were remembered when the Grammar School introduced its house system in 1907. The houses are Sir Walter Mildmay house, Joseph Strutt house, Sir Nicholas Tindal house, and Dr Philemon Holland house. All of these were not only prominent and influential members of the community, but also ex-pupils of the school.

The affordable Ford Pop will bring back fond memories for those who had the pleasure of owning one of these basic, functional cars. The windscreen wiper, pivoted above the windscreen, was replaced in later models, by a vacuum operated one which slowed and stopped as the accelerator was depressed, but swung wildly as the foot was lifted.

Bottom: A glorious summer's day in Moulsham Street. We can just see a single motor vehicle in the far distance but otherwise the road glories in the complete absence of cars. If one were to see so many bicycles today one would immediately assume that some kind of cycle rally was underway but here the cycles parked on either side of the road and being ridden along it make it merely an ordinary day. These were the days before mountain bikes and cycle helmets when many

preferred, or at least professed to prefer, cycling to the shops and to work rather than taking a car. And we could claim to be doing our bit for the environment - or we would have done had anyone then given any thought to it. How many of these cyclists we wonder could have imagined that in not too many years time the road would be clogged with motorcars and that a leisurely cycle to the shops would become a journey fraught with danger? Another significant feature of this photo is the number of sun-blinds which are out - for some reason few shops seem to bother with them these days. In the centre of the scene is the Star and Garter public house: at least if we still take our bicycles to the pub we don't risk of the dreaded breathalyser.

This fascinating view shows St Mary's Church at Great Baddow. The building is by far the oldest structure in the photograph and the extensive churchyard and grounds can clearly be seen leading away from the church to the right. In the days before the area was quite so built up the character of this village was markedly different. Notice the large, almost square property at the bottom right of the scene. This was once the substantial and imposing vicarage, but in later years was converted to flats. Moving left from the vicarage a row of half-timbered houses clings to the edge of the winding road. These have long since been swept

away in the name of progress. The photograph dates from the early 1960s, a time when it was still considered undignified to hang washing out on virtually any day of the week other than Monday (and never on Sunday!). We can draw our own conclusions about when the picture was taken from the time shown on the church clock, the virtual absence of cars and pedestrians in view, and the lines of washing seen flapping in the wind over several neat suburban gardens. Many of these gardens have small outbuildings and greenhouses within their boundaries, reflecting the increasing popularity of gardening as a hobby in postwar Britain.

Left: The Conduit with its cupola cover now resides in Tower Gardens, off Roxwell Road. It was moved in 1940 to make way for the increasing traffic at this junction. It seems that it was always being pushed aside for something else as its usefulness diminished with the years. It had already moved from Tindal Square, previously known as Conduit Square, where this structure had covered the town's water supply from 1814 to 1852. To add to its humiliation it was making way for a statue of Judge Tindal whose name had replaced its own. A further indignity was to use it as a signpost to Colchester, and yet another to attach an early traffic light to one of its columns. Other traffic lights can be seen above the shop roller blinds. It is difficult to work out why the lights have been placed as they have, as there appears to be no control over traffic coming up the street, passing the conduit to the right. It seems unclear as to whether the vehicles coming down Springfield Road should regard the Conduit as a round-about, or proceed as if it was not there.

Perhaps the gentleman wearing the fashionable plus fours, bought them from 'The Fifty Shilling Tailors', which we can see behind him on the corner: two pounds fifty in decimal currency. Many will remember this famous shop, established in the 1920s to provide an affordable suit of clothes. Maybe the gentleman in our picture bought his at Montague Burton's, where soldiers who were 'demobbed', or demobilised, took the vouchers they were given to buy a full suit of clothes. This became known as getting 'the full Monty'!

Above: This delightful view of High Street captures the atmosphere of the bustling commercial centre wonderfully. Nostalgia buffs will delight at the sight of the curvaceous motorcars with their large radiator grilles and lustrous chrome bumpers. The small traffic islands in the middle of High Street were a concession to pedestrian safety, each one an oasis of calm on the precarious journey across the wide and usually very busy roadway. In the distance a canvas banner can be seen tied between two buildings the full width of the street. Keen observers may just be able to make out the message on the advertisement 'Chelmsford Play Reading and Dramatic Club'. The substantial town centre headquarters of the trusty Essex Chronicle is featured on the right hand side of the scene. Here, in the days of 'hot metal', individuals and businessmen would call to book their advertisements and settle their accounts, proud parents would place family announcements, and seasoned reporters and photographers would prepare all the news fit to print for the people of Essex.

Below centre: In September 1959 when this photograph was taken the Cathedral tower was shrouded in scaffolding. The stone and flint edifice was being extensively restored: sixteen unrecognisable carvings beneath the battlements were replaced by a vigorous set of modern carvings by TB Huxley-Jones. An earlier restoration had taken pace in 1932 when it was found that the eight oak timbers could no longer support the old lead cladding which was then replaced by copper to produce the distinctive green colour seen today. The weathervane, now a golden bird with a fanned tail, is a replacement for the earlier weathervane of a flying dragon with a protruding tongue. The picture was taken from Threadneedle Street. HJ Harrison's shop seen in the foreground is now occupied by Beresfords estate agency. A new diocese was created in 1914. The parish of Chelmsford was originally dedicated to St Mary the Virgin. On October 26th 1954 the cathedral was dedicated as the Cathedral Church of St Mary the Virgin, St Peter and St Cedd. St Cedd was a Celtic missionary who died in 654 AD. The three saints are commemorated symbolically in stone in the centre of three faces of the tower with a bishop's mitre in the fourth, whilst the four corners are decorated with a harp, a Saracen's head, a lion and a boar's head taken from the coats of arms of local families.

Essex Libraries

Bottom: From Market Road the Shire Hall looks impressive in the afternoon sunshine in this picture taken in 1957. The Shire Hall was built in 1791 to a design by architect John Johnson, the neo-classical facade has three plaques between its four pillars these depict representations of 'Justice', 'Wisdom' and 'Mercy' fitting aspirations for those involved with public administration. Just inside the doorway is a statue of a naiad or water nymph. The statue of Judge Tindal surveys the scene outside in the square named in his honour, perhaps thinking his own thoughts about the subjects being deliberated by occupants of the chambers within. In times gone by cattle used to be herded through the streets past this spot on their way to the railway goods yard. There is an interesting assortment of means of getting around displayed here. Apart from pedestrians an LD Lambretta may be seen in the bottom right of the picture beside a Riley displaying an AA badge and a place for a hand crank; behind it is what is almost certainly a Ford Popular. Travelling in front of the Shire Hall is a vehicle bearing the distinctive wood trim of a sturdy shooting brake, and the horse trough brings with it echoes of the days when the internal combustion engine existed only in the imagination of those gifted with extraordinary foresight.

Essex Libraries

Memories of **CHELMSFORD**

Essex Libraries

Above: There is little to impede the progress of the Austin Ruby as it makes its way along the High Street in the 1950s. It is passing a pedestrian crossing with its familiar beacons. Whilst the beacons had been in existence for some years, they only began to 'blink' in 1952, and the received their stripes in 1951. Following the war few people could afford to own a car, but by the late fifties and sixties, when the country began to prosper, traffic problems increased. There was some easing of the chaos when the A12 by-pass was opened, but the pressure increased as more and more could afford to buy a car. The High Street became pedestrianised and a new flyover was needed over the Army and Navy roundabout, notorious for its traffic jams. The Saracen's Head has changed little over time, and has outlived the many other Inns which once lined this street. Now they have been converted to hold treasures for the hundreds of shoppers, who benefit from modern street lighting. At the beginning of this consumer age, shops offered many more electrical goods. Record players, essential now for the demanding teenagers, washing machines, cookers and electric kettles, were all on offer. In the fifties more people were discovering the wonders of television. They would return from the shops and stare at the smiling child, who sat in front of the patterned test card and adjust the brightness and contrast controls. The picture often had to be stabilised with the horizontal and vertical controls to stop it from rolling over. This was often done under pressure as the children waited for the first programme of the day, 'Muffin the Mule'. There may well have been the occasional shout of 'Crackerjack', as mum cooked the meal.

Below: The High Street looks pretty enough to decorate any Christmas Card. Do all scenes become more attractive with the passing of the years? The snow was not looked upon in quite so romantic a way in 1881 when it was reported to be as deep as six feet in Baddow Road and Springfield Road.

The Austin car parked at the pavement edge will bring back nostalgic memories of what seem now, with hindsight, to be the Golden Years of motoring. Maybe we have forgotten how easy it was to flood the engine with petrol if we held the choke open too long, or to run the battery flat if we did not apply the right amount of pressure to the accelerator at the right moment to make the engine fire into life. Because of these idiosyncrasies, we talked nicely to them and gave them affectionate names in the hope that they would not let us down. Picture the same scene covered in water instead of snow, and you have an idea of the shock for the people of Chelmsford when the town was flooded on 3rd August 1888. Citizens of the town paddled, up to their knees in the water in the High Street. The rain was so heavy that the resulting flood had sufficient power to wash away the Iron Bridge. Further flooding has occurred more recently. In August 1987 the city was again plagued with flood-water. In October of the same year hurricane force winds damaged buildings and uprooted trees. In the 'Mayor's Avenue' Central Park, the trees toppled like dominoes. Hylands Park lost many trees in what was said to be the worst storm in three hundred years.

Essex Libraries

Left: To be a photographer you need more than a camera and a roll of film. A good head for heights is also essential. This picture was taken from high above on the walkways around the cathedral. Fortunately for the person pointing the lens, the scaffolding around the tower provided some feeling of security. In 1959 the cathedral was undergoing renovation. This was the era of 'Supermac', Prime Minister Harold Macmillan. He told us we had never had it so good. Even our footballers made us proud. Billy Wright had just played 100 times for England. The photographed scene has altered from that time. The area around Duke Street, to the right, where the Corn Exchange stood on the corner of Wells Street, has been redeveloped. Threadneedle Street runs away towards the top of the photograph, with the collection of banks and Market House to its left. Tindal Square, that now boasts the statue of Judge Tindal, is in the centre of the panorama. The photographer might have been humming a few choruses of the popular tunes of 1959 to distract him from any feelings of vertigo. Buddy Holly's 'It doesn't matter any more' would have been particularly poignant if he had slipped. Had he fallen to earth, he could certainly have been said to be 'Travelling light'. No doubt he could have asked the crowd that gathered to watch his demise 'What do you want to make those eyes at me for?'

Below: The developers are having a field day here: Conrad Ritblat of Manchester Square London W1 has bought up four adjacent properties next to the bridge. Amongst the buildings acquired by Conrad Ritblat are E L Hunt Ltd the builders' merchants advertising stoves, baths and paints whilst next door, in the centre of this sad scene, is Leons outfitters. The fact that just one person is seen in this photograph walking past the boarded up shops seems to tell its sorry own tale - that despite the time of day, with other shops open in the distance their blinds down against the sunlight, nevertheless this bit of town is dead, awaiting some new development to breath life into it. Just over the bridge can be seen Pearl Assurance House whilst on the far right almost out of frame are the first two letters of the word 'Hovis' the wholemeal bread that at one time seemed to be the only brown bread one could buy before roughage in one's diet became fashionable rather than just a secret shared amongst the ultra health conscious. Perhaps the feature which most dates this picture however is the 'street furniture' In this instance the give-away sign is the one atop the black and white pole outside Leons which lists parking restrictions in the days before double yellow lines.

The River Chelmer meanders unobtrusively around the top right hand corner of this aerial view, while from bottom left, Moulsham Street, curving up and round and turning into High Street, provides a through route for north-south traffic. By the junction with Springfield Road, hawk-eyed readers might even be able to pick out a bus passing the Cupola. On this photograph it is possible to distinguish a number of individual buildings which, for one reason and another, have disappeared from the face of Chelmsford - such as the Weslyan Chapel, directly to the left of the highly visible, round, white object, which is in fact the circus tent. If we move down a little way from a point midway between the Chapel and the tent, stopping before we reach Baddow Road, we can see the long roof of the Tannery. Baddow Road gave access to the side door of the cinema; many cinema-goers used to leave their bikes here - and find them still there, complete with front wheel, when they came out after the film! Immediately above the Chapel, up beyond Springfield Road, is the Brewery. The Black Boy pub is on Springfield Road itself, near the junction with High Street. Heading out of town, to the right, we pass the spot where the Empire Cinema, known as the Flea-Pit, burned down before the war.

Essex Libraries

Above: The Ford Popular and Mini are turning by the Belisha beacon at Baddow Road Corner. They were two of the best loved cars of that time. The 'Pop' followed a long line of affordable cars that included the Ford 8, the Prefect and the larger Zephyr. The Mini came on the scene in 1959. It was the brainchild of Alex Issigonis, a designer who had worked on the introduction of the Morris Minor in 1948. The boxy, inexpensive, fuel-efficient Mini used a transverse engine to power its front wheels. That was a radical design at the time. It could comfortably seat four passengers despite being only 10 feet long. The cars are passing Lovedays, the jeweller. What a wonderful name for courting couples to pause under as they admired the engagement rings on display in the shop window. Their days of love would be cemented by a token bought from a shop with an appropriately romantic name. The jeweller occupied the ground floor of the C & S building that dated from 1896. On the other side of the road, by the railings, the aroma of cooking wafted pleasantly on the breeze. The Kingfisher fish and chip shop did good business. Freshly cooked cod and crispy chips, with the vinegar soaking into the newspaper, bring back memories of fingers being stung. Salt got into any little paper cut on our hands, but it was glorious to be able to lick your fingers clean as the last scraps disappeared. They don't taste the same out of a polystyrene tray.

Essex Libraries

Above right: The big names in retailing have begun to line up along High Street, while in the distance, the hoardings mark the spot where the Weslyan Chapel had stood prior to the clearance of the site for redevelopment. The whole 'shopping experience' changed enormously over the course of the 20th century. In the early 1900s, neighbouring towns felt little need to compete with one another for custom. Journeys of any distance were a major undertaking, and the notion of travelling from Chelmsford to London just for a shopping trip would have seemed quite outrageous to all but the most wealthy. Indeed, it was the norm for tailors and other tradesmen to visit their customers' residences. You would, for instance, be measured for your new dress or suit at home, and it would be delivered to you when it was ready. No popping into Burton's for off-the-peg, mix-and-match outfits in those days! As the self-service trend became established during the middle decades of the 20th century, we began to enjoy wandering in and out of the town's various clothes stores, trying on garments that caught our eye. In this photograph Burton's, along with Woolworths, Phillips' shoe shop, Tesco and their neighbours provided the most modern shopping experience of the day, but even that was to change before too long, when pedestrian streets and shopping centres became the order of the day.

Memories of CHELMSFORD

Below centre: A view of Stone Bridge or Bishop's Bridge as it is sometimes known on Springfield Road. The date 1787 is shown on the keystone in the centre of the bridge and it was around this crossing of the River Can that Chelmsford grew up. So many towns owe their prosperity and significance to the fact that they were situated at the most convenient point to get across rivers. The Iron Bridge situated further left of this site was erected in 1890 to replace the one washed away in the flood of 1888. The imposing structure of the Wesleyan Chapel built in 1847 has been subsequently demolished and been replaced by Cater's Stores. Many such chapels up and down the country have suffered the same fate or have been turned into carpet warehouses; but in its heyday it served a thriving worshipping community and the Sunday School built at the rear accommodated around 300 children every week. We are not sure of the date this photograph was taken but the length of the hemline worn by the lady about to go over the bridge suggests the late 1950s or early 1960s before the shock or thrill of the miniskirt (depending on your point of view) had disturbed the calm of Essex's county town. What is certain is that the scene pictured here is considerably quieter as regards the volume of traffic than the present day equivalent.

Essex Libraries

Bottom: It may be five to ten in the morning in June 1961 but by the look of the women's coats in this scene the weather was far from flaming. On the left of the frame the Corn Exchange can just be seen. Opposite the camera, to the right of Duke Street, are, from left to right, Cobbe & Wincer, Godfrey's and Debenhams stores. The wonderful thing about this photograph is, like so many in this collection, the virtual absence of motor cars: the only car in view is safely parked. In an important sense this picture typifies not merely Chelmsford but much of Britain with its extraordinary mixture of architectural styles, a mish-mash of buildings which fascinates foreign visitors and is sometimes seen as a blessing and at others as a curse. Such a mixture of styles can be seen in many towns and cities throughout England and in this instance is wonderfully illustrated in the contrast between the venerable spired cathedral tower in the background which is partly framed by the modern office block on the left, the Italianate Corn Exchange and the higgledy-piggledy sky-line made by the roofs of the three shops in the foreground.

Essex Libraries

This picture of High Street featuring the Saracens Head Hotel so prominently in the foreground was taken around 1968. We could readily make a guess at the date of this scene even if we did not already know it: the sight of Hillman Imps, Ford Anglias and Bedford vans immediately takes us back to the swinging sixties, to the music of the Beatles and the Rolling Stones, not to mention Harold Wilson's Labour Government and beer still only around two shillings a pint for those of us old enough to get served in pubs. One of the other things which also readily gives away the decade is the length of

Essex Libraries

hemlines, with the mini-skirt, which had shocked so many on its first appearance, now a regular feature of the streets to the gratification of menfolk of all ages. How many accidents have been caused by drivers staring for rather too long at mini clad girls has never been recorded, but there is no doubt that more than one cyclist in those helmetless days came to grief as a result of the distractions afforded by the fair sex. And it was not just cyclists who were less safety conscious than their modern counterparts: just note the lorry carrying a load of sacks in the left hand lane of traffic and its precariously balanced load!

Essex Libraries

Above: Standing in glorious isolation in 1965, the Corn Exchange awaits its demolition. It was built in 1857 to a design by Frederic Chancellor, the first mayor of Chelmsford, whose name is now given to modern buildings near this site. It was to this place that the Charter of Incorporation was brought from London. A band greeted the members of the council on their return from London, and a large crowd gathered outside waving Union Jacks and giving three cheers to Queen Victoria as the charter was held high on the balcony of the Corn Exchange. Within living memory Mr McVeigh taught ballroom dancing in rooms on the first floor, where this historical event had taken place. Before 'Rock and Roll' the grace and manners of ballroom dancing were essentials skills for a young man to master. Many romances blossomed to the strains of Victor Sylvester and his Orchestra as they moved around the floor to a waltz, quickstep or a slow Fox trot. Perhaps the most important sentence ever used by a boy, who wished to get to know a particular girl, was, 'May I have the pleasure of this dance?' Unlike dance forms which came after, the boy had an instant opportunity to hold her in his arms.

Mr McVeigh and Mr C P Freeman, who contributed much to the information in this book, both served in the 11th Battalion of the Essex Home-guard. Previously known as Local Defence Volunteers, they were later renamed the Home Guard. Affectionately known as 'Dad's Army', they performed many essential duties. In an emergency they were called from their other full time reserved occupations.

Right: The drivers of these buses on the Danbury route along the A414 must have been heartily sick of turning the corner by Lloyd's Bank from Duke Street into Broomfield Road. They knew they were going to be faced with another slow and frustrating journey. The traffic congestion in the 1960s was reaching ridiculous proportions. Britain was enjoying a period of affluence. It showed. The motor car, once a luxury, was now a necessity. The roads were clogged with lines of traffic as drivers fought for their own little bit of space. Older bus drivers had seen it all before. In 1947 they had threatened to go on strike if the congestion on the roads was not sorted out. That was in a time of petrol rationing when traffic was comparatively light when compared to this scene. One way of easing the journey around town had been explored by the driver of the little car in the centre of the picture. He was in a BMW Issetta, the contraption nicknamed the 'bubble car'. Likened by some to a front loading washing machine on wheels, this motor car was designed with ease of parking and manoeuvrability in mind. It was popular with long legged models who could pose for photographers as they got out of one. However, its lack of real street cred and vulnerability in an accident meant that the bubble car was a passing fad. In 1985 the British inventor, Clive Sinclair, tried something similar when he introduced the tiny, battery operated C5. That was even less successful.

During the early 1960s many people began to discover the delights of being stuck inside a tin box in slow-moving, nose-to-tail traffic on a hot summer's day. This scene, looking along Duke Street, was captured by the camera on 14th August, 1962. Car ownership at that time was escalating rapidly. Just under a decade earlier, in 1953, one adult in every twenty-four, nationwide, had owned a car. Ten years later, in 1963, one adult in seven was a car owner. The trend was to continue, of course. In 1967 there were over ten million cars on Britain's roads, more than double the number there had been in 1957. Clearly, town centres had to take action. Before too long, most, like Chelmsford, opted for pedestrian zones, one-way streets and traffic systems which kept cars away from the shopping streets. At first there was a tendency to regard such new-fangled ideas with some suspicion, perhaps considering them too radical, and rather a nuisance. But it was not long before we became enthusiastic about pedestrian precincts - not only did they offer practical advantages, but they could potentially be made very attractive, and they became quite a feature of the 1960s. Those of us who went up to London regularly around the time of this photograph may well remember visiting Carnaby Street, the trendiest, hippest pedestrian zone of them all.

At leisure

This would have been quite a novelty for the thirteen men perched precariously on top of this early public transport vehicle. The photograph is thought to date from 1910 and was taken outside the White Hart in Chelmsford to record the inauguration of the first open motorbus in the whole of Essex. For many of the men featured here even having one's photograph taken would have been something to talk about. The men are carefully turned out in their collars and ties, with watch chains and the particular style of hat worn indicating their place in the social pecking order. Thomas Clarkson pioneered the first vehicle of this type and in doing so brought employment to many local people. His firm grew to be a leading player in the world of steam powered vehicles, though as we now know, the steam powered vehicle concept did not endure. The National Steam Car Company was a major customer of Clarksons and operated a fleet of vehicles in London between 1909 and 1919. At it's peak the fleet numbered 184, such was the scale of the firm's activities.

Essex Libraries

Left: Charringtons beers have long since disappeared from this site; the Essex Arms in Springfield Road having ceased to be a pub and become an Indian restaurant. Springfield Road from Victoria Road to the top of Springfield Hill always had something of a village street atmosphere - from Jim Copsey's butcher's shop, which once stood at the corner of Victoria Road opposite the Three Cups hardware store, past the cycle shop and private houses as far as the Essex Arms. This undated photograph appears to have been taken in the mid 1960s. Outside the pub we can see a Vespa scooter - the name means 'wasp' in Italian, an appropriate name from the whine of its high revving engine compared to the full throated roar of famous British motor cycles such as BSA and Triumph. The future of road transport is represented by the A35 shooting brake parked next to the scooter, whilst resolutely clinging to a more traditional form of transport is a gentleman on his bicycle, his socks safely tucked into trousers; he is riding a solid reliable bike with good wide mud guards and sensible handle bars. For obvious reasons we cannot see it, but the chances are that he would be sitting on a broad leather double-sprung Rudge saddle which made up for what it may have lacked in style by being probably the most comfortable bicycle saddle ever made.

Above: An historic picture of The Old Black Boy inn in Springfield Road with its intricate wrought iron sign. The 'Fine Ales and Stout' from the local Ridley brewery are advertised on the signs across the facade. Its main point of interest according to the photo is its Saloon Bar but it is reputed to have been a lodging place for Charles Dickens when it served as a boarding house for travellers on the main Colchester to London Road. The pub is now no longer there but it is commemorated by a heritage Blue Plaque stating that this was the site of the Old Black Boy Inn. Unfortunately for those concerned with historical accuracy it is displayed on the wrong building. The site is now occupied by a branch of the Next chain of stores and a branch of Habitat is situated a little further down the street. The adjacent building remains today and is significant as it was, at the time this photograph was taken, used by Ridley's Brewery. The door on the upper level as well as the hoist may still be seen today and beer is still brewed by Ridley's in the time honoured tradition as it was when the patrons of the Old Black Boy enjoyed their pints at their 'local'. The proximity of the pub to the brewery would ensure that there were always fresh supplies of ale available. The car making its way down the road is a Standard 8 or 10.

Above: In 1920 when this photograph was taken Chelmsford's Central Park was still known simply as the Recreation Grounds. The area is now divided in two by a major road - the aptly named Parkway. This idyllic summer scene readily conjures up the scent of the flowers laid out in beds in the foreground whilst the innocence of the young girl pushing her coach built doll's pram takes us back to an earlier, happier time when children's ideas of what might constitute a suitable birthday gift or Christmas present didn't include computers or video recorders. In those now long gone days children were still taught that they should be seen and not heard and although ball games were permitted woe betide those who strayed from the designated areas; they would soon find themselves being chased by an irate park keeper. During the second world war the 211 Rocket Battery was located here with anti-aircraft guns manned by the 101 Essex Homeguard. In the north west corner of the Recreation Ground a barrage balloon was tethered to prevent more low level air raids which had earlier been aimed at Hoffman's engineering works. It is not however just events of the second world war which are called to mind by this picture, in the distance, to the right of the flower bedecked band-stand, can be seen a first world war tank!

Right: The approach to the market is very quiet on this day in June 1961. There is very little traffic on the move as pedestrians make their unhurried way along the road. This was the year when the one millionth Morris Minor was produced, and not a one in sight! It was the first British car to reach the magical seven-figure number. When it was first produced as a two-door saloon it cost £280. In 1961 it sold for the sum of £416, a price that the manufacturers claimed was relatively less than its original price.

Early in the history of Market Road, pedestrians would have found that the traffic, which they encountered then, was the four-legged variety. Cattle and sheep were driven down this road to pens at the bottom of the road to the left. To the right was the poultry market. We can imagine the noises of the animals and the auctioneers and traders. On the right of the picture were the premises of traders selling farm equipment. After a day's trading the animals were herded back up the road through Tindal Square and along the streets to the railway goods yard. For many years there was a water trough alongside the statue of Judge Tindal, for the benefit of animals. The road surface would not have been as comfortable underfoot as these pedestrians experienced in 1961. It was one of the duties of the first paid firemen, who were stationed in a building in this road, to wash the road and keep the area clean.

Essex Libraries

Below: Swimming was good for you - whether you liked it or not. Just like the cod liver oil administered to small boys and girls to provide the much needed vitamins lacking in the diet during the war. School milk was distributed before playtime in schools, and many a 'flying saucer' was made from the foil tops. It was now considered important to develop the body as well as the mind, and Physical Education developed as the grander form of 'drill'. There was an assumption that children by nature enjoyed games and other strenuous activities. Certificates were issued when the first length of the pool was conquered. Then came the life saving badges. There was always a fabric badge, which was stitched with black thread and pride to the front of the swimming costume. These awards were, for many, the only enjoyable aspect of the whole experience as the emphasis was on learning to survive and there seemed to be no place for fun. The children here at the open-air pool seem to be enjoying the experience, where pleasure is the driving force. Chelmsford's pool, in Waterloo Lane, is designed. with fun. as well as health in mind. Children's screams of pleasure can be heard as they hurtle down water slides, which twist and turn. After a swim, children today can visit bright cafes serving all manner of goodies. Much better that the sandy cocoa offered to children in the 50s when they emerged shivering from the pool with their chlorine red eyes. In 1986 it was extended to include an ice-rink, sports hall, health centre, multi-gym, squash courts and many other features including something called 'kool kids' - that sounds like fun!

Bottom: Going back to school in September 1953 had its good points. For one thing, there was Story Hour to look forward to. The group pictured here in the Children's Library on 29th October, 1953 is listening to Ms AG Royce read them stories - wonderful tales about that loveable Bear of Very Little Brain, and the fantastic adventures of Jack and the Beanstalk. Many new characters have joined the ranks of the heroes and heroines of children's literature since this photograph was taken, and readers with children, grandchildren and even great-grandchildren of their own will have seen various crazes come and go. Children have whole worlds full of adventure to choose from - cowboys and pirates, secret agents and gangsters, mysterious masked heroes, sorcerers, fairy princesses, dinosaurs and space aliens. Only time will tell which books are destined to turn into true children's classics, enchanting generation after generation of young readers. Certainly Winnie-the-Pooh, Piglet, Eeyore and friends have stood the test of time, as have Peter Rabbit, Alice, Thomas the Tank Engine, Ratty and Toad in The Wind in the Willows ... no doubt we all have our own special favourites. Even if we can't recall the name of the girl or boy we sat next to at primary school, the chances are we will remember the friends we met and spent many happy hours with, between the covers of books.

How dignified Chelmsford's Pavilion Cinema, in Rainsford Road, looked in the early 1920s, with its grand, decorated frontage set off nicely against the leafy backdrop! Cinema was a hugely popular entertainment at this time. All over Britain new cinemas were being built, and former music hall theatres were converted into picture-houses as the silver screen enticed audiences away from the stage. Cinema-goers were entertained not only by the moving pictures but also by the showmanship and panache of the cinema organist, playing, as often as not, a Wurlitzer. Early silent movie stars included such legendary figures as Charlie Chaplin and Rudolf Valentino. The first 'talkie' was the 1927 film 'The Jazz Singer', which did not have a full sound-track but did contain songs and snatches of dialogue. More mature readers may remember Al Jolson's tremendous rendition of the song 'Danny Boy' in 'The Singing Fool' the following year. Great British movie directors of the era included Alfred Hitchcock, who in 1929 brought us 'Blackmail', the first full-length talking picture to be made in Britain. On a different note, the Pavilion's noticeboard carries two flyers below the film posters, upon which - with the aid of a magnifying glass - the words 'Ireland's Parliament' can be picked out. This is another, rather more sinister sign of the times, as the early 1920s were an era of bitter dispute over Lloyd George's creation of the Irish Free State.

Essex Libraries

Essex Libraries

on the right, with its blinds still down, to buy a packet of Senior Service cigarettes advertised on the wall above; in those days one could still smoke at the cinema: it was to be some years yet before no smoking seats were introduced followed inevitably by no smoking at all.

Top: Next door to the pork sausages and pies, the Regent was showing 'Blind Date'. Cilla Black was not turning up to a special premiere near Baddow Road Corner. This was before she started her pop singing career. Her TV dating programme and a 'lorra, lorra laughs' was a long way off. This 'Blind Date' was a British film released in 1959. It starred Hardy Kruger and two actors who

Above: The number 11 Chelmsford bus has just stopped to allow passengers to disembark to visit the cinema here in Baddow Road. The Odeon in Baddow Road, part of a massive national chain of cinemas, is featuring Max Bygraves in a film called 'Spare the Rod'. It may not have won any Oscars, but at least was made in Britain. The word 'Odeon' incidentally comes from the name for a theatre in ancient Greece. Not everyone caught the bus of course and those lucky enough to own their own cars could park with ease; even right outside the cinema. Those really were the days, before traffic clogged our roads and parking one's car became a nightmare with yellow lines painted along almost every street in town. On the right of the scene, barely visible is the Nag's Head pub where those who had worked up a thirst at the cinema could pop in for a drink before catching the last bus home. Perhaps too, those who were going to the Odeon had called at the shop

appeared in supporting roles in dozens of movies, Stanley Baker and Gordon Jackson. The black and white film had a story line that sounds rather racy for the time. A young Dutch painter discovers the body of his mistress and finds himself in a web of deceit. Sadly, the murder mystery was fairly glum with an uninteresting plot. But that would not have worried cinema-goers as the swinging 60s were about to unfold. They enjoyed a Saturday night at the pictures because it was good value for money. There were two feature films, a cartoon and the Pathé newsreel to enjoy. The programme was continuous, so people often arrived part way through a film and watched the beginning later. This may sound an odd way of doing things. Audiences seemed quite happy to know the end of a story and discover how it had all begun later on. Anyway, for many the film was not important. They had some serious courting to do on the back row.

The triple string of pearls, the brooch, the full length coat and feathery hat in powder blue, coupled with the regal bearing and the warm smile were hallmarks of the much-loved Queen Elizabeth the Queen Mother as far back as this visit she paid to Chelmsford in February 1962. The local paper of Friday 2 March 1962 declared that 'the royal visit was most successful.... Despite snow earlier on in the morning and a bitter wind which kept a lot of people away, many saw the helicopter arrive and the royal visit ran entirely to schedule'. She was welcomed to the town by Sir John Ruggles-Brise, Lord Lieutenant of Essex, who escorted her to the County High School where she was shown round by the then Headmistress Miss Pattison. They later went on to the Odeon Cinema, Baddow Road, where HRH gave prizes and certificates at the school's Speech Day. Not all the pupils gaining awards on that occasion were honoured by being presented to Her Majesty, however. No little upset was caused by the decision to have only 75 girls receive their certificates from the royal visitor, the rest were to be given them at the door by the school secretary. This provoked much anger from parents. After giving a 10 minute address HRH was thanked by the Mayor Ald Mrs Jean Roberts, pictured here walking beside the Queen Mother outside the Civic Centre.

Events & occasions

A radiant Queen Mother signs the Distinguished Visitors Book in the Mayor's Parlour on 23 February 1962. Standing next to HRH, wearing the chains of mayoral office, stands Ald Mrs Jean P Roberts who is accompanied by her husband Cllr LF Roberts. The gentleman on the right of the picture is the then Town Clerk Mr BA Francis. Her Majesty arrived in the town by helicopter, landing in the grounds of the County High School and departed in the same manner from Melbourne Park. Fourteen members of the Borough Council had the honour of being presented to HRH during this visit. She also met Mr Richard Evans who was Keeper of the Civic Centre at the time; earlier in his life he had served as steward on the 'Queen Mary' when her Majesty was returning from her tour of Canada in 1954. A letter to the editor of the local paper printed the week following the visit expressed surprised that no one had helped the Queen Mother alight from the helicopter, as this would have been a demonstration of good manners. Evidence of a certain ambivalence as to what exactly constituted 'good manners' can be seen from the fact that the alternative view was expressed that the offer of assistance in such circumstances could easily be construed in the opposite way. How Her Majesty viewed the situation will probably never be known. It was an eventful time in Chelmsford - only the week before the royal visit the statue of Judge Tindal had been removed for cleaning after it had watched over the comings and goings in the town centre for 112 years.

Above: There was tremendous excitement in Chelmsford in April 1963 when Her Majesty Queen Elizabeth and HRH Prince Philip visited the town for the age-old tradition of distributing the Royal Maundy Money. Crowds began to form two hours before the official arrival time of 11.23 am, and by 10.30 am people were standing up to seven deep in places along the well-publicised route. Preparations for the visit were extremely thorough with every road and pavement along the way receiving a pre-visit spring-clean and every civic official rehearsing his or her part in the proceedings until perfection was achieved. It was estimated that 5000 loyal subjects turned out to support the royal couple on the streets of Chelmsford. Extra police officers were drafted in from surrounding districts to control the enthusiasm of the cheering throng, and many of the more experienced Bobbies took the opportunity to show off their wartime decorations on the day. The royal couple had earlier flown into Stanstead airport to be met by Lt. Col. NR Salew and the Chief Constable of Essex. They left under close motor escort for the relatively short drive to Chelmsford at 10.45 am, the glittering motorcade wafting effortlessly through each junction on the journey as traffic policemen saluted while holding other road users at bay.

Right: In the hour or so before the royal party arrived in Chelmsford civic dignitaries and other guests began arriving for the Maundy ceremony at the Cathedral. Her Majesty's ceremonial bodyguard, The Yeoman of the Guard, in their splendid scarlet and gold costumes were among the first to take their places. A procession of civic officials from all over Essex soon followed. The mayors and mayoresses of all the other County boroughs were in attendance, along with their town clerks. The Chairman of Essex County Council, Ald. Sir George Chaplin, and the High Sheriff of Essex Colonel H Hunter James led the civic party to the cathedral where 10 young members of Her Majesty's Chapel Royal choir sang with the choir of Chelmsford Cathedral. As the guests and Maundy recipients arrived at the cathedral photographers snapped away as the crowds looked on with mounting excitement in anticipation of the arrival of the royal VIPs.

Above: White gloves were the order of the day for the 400 police officers drafted in to assist the local force on the day of the royal visit. These young police officers would remember this day for decades to come, as would the crowds of people who had abandoned their shopping (and, in some cases, their shops) in order to catch a glimpse of the popular monarch. For some, such as the old soldiers seen on the right representing the British Legion, the occasion had a more poignant significance as memories of military ceremonies and absent friends were brought to the fore. The timing of visit had been meticulous, right down to the last minute. There was a hush at 11.23 am when the royal motorcade was scheduled to arrive in Tindal Square. Two minutes later - perhaps the longest two minutes endured by the waiting officials - the gleaming black limousines glided silently into view. The roar made by the waiting throng had to be experienced to be believed. Hundreds of union flags stirred the air as people went wild with excitement and the royal car came to a halt. The whole of Rainsford Road, Duke Street and Tindal Square had been lined with passionate supporters who now wanted to get closer to the Cathedral and its royal guests. The mood was good humoured throughout and the police worked quietly and efficiently to ensure the safety of the swirling masses as the ceremony progressed unseen.

Above right: The enviable honour of greeting the Queen and Prince Philip in Tindal Square fell upon the Mayor of Chelmsford Ald. Mrs MM Davies and the Town Clerk Mr BA Francis. An immaculate blue carpet had been laid for the occasion to protect the royal footsteps en-route to the cathedral. Necks were craned among members of the now hushed crowds as people strained to see what Her Majesty was wearing and just what exactly was going on during the first few minutes of her visit. Those lucky enough to have an open view of the proceedings saw that the Queen was wearing a fashionable mid blue semi-fitted coat and a blue and green featherbed domed hat and pale blue accessories. Murmers ebbed and flowed around the assembled masses as descriptions and opinions about Her Majesty's attire circulated through the gathering. Everyone agreed that their Queen was at least as beautiful as they had hoped, and that this was an occasion they wouldn't have missed for the world.

By the time this scene was captured the congregation and honoured guests had already assembled in Chelmsford Cathedral for the Maundy Service. Her Majesty was escorted into the cathedral by the Very Reverend G Eric Gordon, the Lord Provost of Chelmsford, closely followed by Prince Philip and the Lord Lieutenant of Essex Colonel Sir John Ruggles-Brise. In the ceremony that followed the queen presented the Royal Maundy Money to deserving local people. Traditionally, the number of recipients is the same number of men, and women, as the Sovereign has years of age. In 1963 this number was 37. During the ceremony Her Majesty presented each female recipient with a small green purse containing £1 15s 0d - £1.75 in modern currency. Each of the 37 male recipients was given a white purse containing £25s 0d - or £2.25 in 'modern' money. The ages of the people concerned ranged between 65 and 90 years. Observers said that the women were seen to curtsey politely and beam with gratitude, while most of the men bowed their heads in sombre respect. It was a day that none of them would ever forget. During the Maundy service the choir sang an anthem from Zadok the Priest before the whole congregation enthusiastically sang the National Anthem. Later the Queen was entertained to lunch at the Civic Centre where she signed the visitors book in the Council Chamber and met members of the council.

S tanding in the sunshine beneath the Union flag fluttering in the gentle breeze, civic and military dignitaries line up outside the Civic Centre housed in the old library to welcome HRH Princess Margaret to the town on Tuesday 24 April 1973. She came in her role as Deputy Colonel in Chief of the Royal Anglian Regiment to open the Essex Regiment Museum in Oaklands Park. The main purpose of her visit was to unveil a commemorative plaque in the Essex Regiment Museum a new gallery, built onto the Chelmsford and Essex Museum to house the military collection from Warley Barracks. The collection traces the story of the regiment through the 200 years of its independent history before it was incorporated into the Royal Anglian Regiment in 1964. Many children eager to get a good view of the royal visitor perched on the cannon in Oaklands Park. If possible those involved in the planning of the event would have organised weather like this, so there were many sighs of relief on that account; however not all the arrangements went as satisfactorily and some last minute changes were necessary when illness prevented Major Tom Stead, the regimental secretary of the Royal Anglian, who along with former Borough Librarian Eric Reed had done a great deal of hard work to set up the museum, from being present. His place was taken by Major David Purves, a former commanding officer of the no. 3 Company, the 5th Battalion of the Royal Anglian Regiment.

The 1950s and the wonder and excitement of the acquisition of the first television set. Black and white of course and though this model was not one of the cheapest sets available then, the screen was probably only a modest twelve or fourteen inches. People then considered television a mere adjunct of radio and even the design of this set makes it look like a wireless. It may well have been acquired to enable the family (and others) to watch the Queen's Coronation in 1953. The dress of the young ladies admiring the set epitomises the 1950s, as does the small table lamp standing on its own mat - so as not to damage this expensive and prized new piece of furniture.

Below (both pictures): It was possibly the acute wartime shortages of food and supplies which made doctors, health workers and mothers alike very aware of the health of the new generation, and children were carefully weighed, measured and immunised against the illnesses that had at one time meant disfigurement or even death. A vaccine for polio, the scourge of former years which left behind its terrible mark of wasted and useless limbs, only came later, however. American scientist Jonas Edward Salk developed a vaccine in 1955, and an oral vaccine was produced in 1960. The vaccines brought the dreaded disease under control and today polio is rarely seen. On a day to day basis, vitamins were vital to the health of children, and long before the advent of the cod liver oil capsule, the recommended spoonful of cod liver oil was administered to the youngest children every day in schools and nurseries around the country during the 1940s. Children might have screwed up their noses at the fishy taste, but the nourishing cod liver oil went a long way towards keeping them healthy. The vitamin-packed orange juice was far more palatable, and artful mothers would often use the orange juice as a bribe: no cod liver oil, no orange juice. Following hard on the heels of the oil, the juice took away the distinctive taste that was disliked by so many children. Ante-natal clinics did all they could to check on the diet, blood

pressure and vitamin intake of mothers to be; our carefully posed photograph, taken in an ante-natal clinic in the 1930s, records at least the cleanliness and tidiness that was to their great credit. And when the tiny new citizen finally arrived, there were health visitors to pay friendly calls on families in their homes to check on the health and happiness of mothers and babies. National Dried Milk for babies was also made available to mothers, and before today's push towards natural feeding NDM was for decades very much in vogue. We need to remember that at the time of these photographs the National Health service did not exist, and in fact the NHS only came into operation after World War II in July 1948.

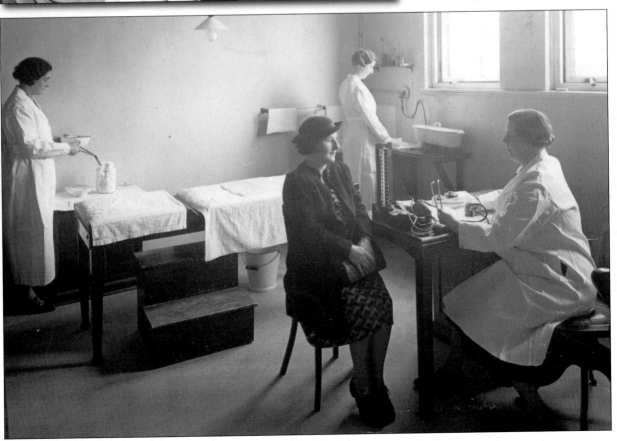

Right: Younger readers may well be astonished to see these ladies seated around the table with their hats on. It was however quite usual for ladies to keep hats on when eating out, even when they took their coats off. In this case, though, the visitors have

Essex Libraries

kept their coats on as well, which rather suggests that this March day was a chilly one. In fact this very civilised tea party took place in the Civic Centre on Tuesday 14th March, 1967. The presence of the Mayor, Alderman Cyril Allsop, and the Mayoress, Mrs K Liddle, indicates that it was an occasion of some significance. The party was being held to celebrate the first anniversary of a scheme introduced by the WRVS to take library books to housebound readers. Over the years the WRVS, formerly the WVS, has found countless ways to serve the community. To many, the WRVS means, first and foremost, a hot drink and a helping hand in times of crisis. During the war, the Service earned the gratitude of thousands for its valiant work, manning the tea vans at all hours of day and night, knitting countless comforters for the troops, and the thousand and one other tasks it performed. The

organisation stayed active as ever after the war, responding to disasters such as fire and flood, and finding practical ways of making life better for children, old folk and others in need.

Below: Members of Chelmsford's Salvation Army are seen proudly marching along Moulsham Street with the Salvation Army Citadel in the background. The picture dates from the early 1960s. The organisation is respected throughout the world for its work in the areas of social service and social reform, but is best known for its vigorously promoted Christian and evangelical beliefs. The Salvation Army was formed in London by William Booth in 1865 and initially known as the Christian Revival Association. Five years later it was renamed the East London Christian Mission, adopting its present name in 1878. The Salvation Army operates in the four corners of the globe and is renowned for the dedication of its members and its rousing brass bands. Officials take military titles and their weekly publication, The War Cry, promotes Christianity wherever it is sold.

Essex Libraries

Essex Libraries

Essex Libraries

Above: Chelmsford has always been proud of the prestige of having the Assizes held in the city. It is reflected in the pomp and ceremony of the escort provided for them as they make their way to the court in Shire Hall. No doubt the police presence is a necessary element, but the sense of occasion is not lost. In early prints of the processing of the judges, in the days of the stagecoach, they would progress up the High Street, from their lodgings flanked by a uniformed mounted escort, the coachman and assistant sitting high in front and two grooms standing or seated behind.

There must have been a little friction between the High Sheriff of Essex and the judges, or maybe he was genuinely concerned at the rising cost of keeping them in rented accommodation, but when the House of Correction was moved from the High Street he suggested that it might well, with a little alteration, provide suitable lodgings for the judges. They were not amused it seems. Eventually they found better rooms higher up the High Street (at what is now the site of number

73). Eventually they were found rooms in a house in New Street. From there they would move, in a dignified way along the path by the Cathedral and into the Shire Hall. The church collapsed on Friday 17th January 1800 between the hours of nine and ten at night. The disaster was blamed on workmen who had been digging between two piers in the south arcade to an open vault, and inadvertently undermined the piers.

Top: Resplendent in their ceremonial robes, the official party gathered on the steps of Central Library on Wednesday 10 April 1935. It was the occasion of the official opening ceremony. The mayor, Councillor SC Taylor, led it. The then mayor, Councillor Hugh Wright MBE, laid the foundation stone for the new library in Duke Street on 25 October 1933. The building was erected by Ashford Builders at a cost of £24,394. It was built on the former site of a private hotel and house. The main library was situated on the ground floor. There was a special area for children's books, a librarians' room, reference room and general reading room. The mayoral parlour was established on the first floor. This large suite was given a waiting room and reception hall. The council chamber, with connecting councillors' waiting and robing rooms, was designed on what were described as 'palatial lines'. The furnishings and fittings of the parlour cost over £1,000, a tidy sum before the war. The old library on Market Road had served Chelmsford since 1904. It held 3,000 books and made 40,000 loans each year. But better education and a thirst for reading material meant that demand outstripped supply. The old library was taken over by the School of Art and Technology. The new one continued to grow and now has 25,000 books in stock. Over 200,000 issues are made annually for home reading.

We believe this photograph to have been taken in or around 1960 - and this is certainly borne out by the hairdo of the lady who is presenting her reader's ticket to Miss G Wade at the issuing desk of the lending library. The 1960s are remembered by many as the era of pop music, pop art and pop culture in general, and to some degree this extends to books as well. Fiction during the 1950s had developed a strong streak of gritty realism, with *angry young men* such as playwright John Osborne coming to the fore to attack what they saw as middle-class values, and novelists Alan Sillitoe and John Braine depicting the bleak reality of working-class life. So, if it's fiction they're after, these borrowers might be taking out The Loneliness of the Long Distance Runner or Room at the Top. Alternatively, the Information Board behind them draws attention to the varied range of special interests which the Library caters for - from Rugby and Middle Distance Running, to Trout Fishing and Chess. Television was of course beginning to have an impact on the nation's reading habits around this time, with an increasing number of people spending their evenings at home in front of the TV instead of curled up with a book. In 1960 there were 10.5 million television sets in Britain, and by 1968 there were 19 million.

Below: School parties are taken on all sorts of educational visits. They go to historical sites, ancient monuments and field study centres. The museum is one of the best places to go. Chelmsford Museum is one of the most interesting for such an outing. It has so much to offer under one roof. This group of well scrubbed youngsters had come on Friday 13 December 1968. They had been prepared for the visit by doing classroom work on the history of the fire brigade. They learned that full time brigades did not become widespread until the 1930s. They listened to their teacher telling them that in 1935 all personnel were trained in anti-gas precautions, just in case war ever broke out. In 1938, as the storm clouds gathered over Europe, the Auxiliary fire service was formed. When hostilities did break out three stations were set up in Chelmsford. They were at Springfield, Rainsford End and New Writtle Street. Armed with this information and their clipboards the children boarded the bus taking them to the museum. Some child was always travel sick and another wanted to know when it was dinner time. Despite those distractions they arrived at the room holding the month-long County Brigade exhibition. It had been running since 16 November 1968. The man in front of the entrance to the bird room explained the differences between the museum hand-pump engine - to the right of the photograph - and a light, modern pump. The children then went back to school to complete to their project work.

Bottom: There will be no joke about the lady seeming 'armless' for she is a graceful figure who dignified the water conduit in the centre of the town for many years. The supply of water came from Burgess' Well, which is now somewhere beneath the Civic Centre car park. It was carried through wooden pipes into the square, where Judge Tindal's statue now stands. Plans of Chelmsford in the 1600s show a channel running from the conduit down the middle of Tindal Street. The water from the conduit would have been used for many purposes, including damping down dusty roads in the height of summer. It would have given refreshment to the horses and livestock being driven to the market. In those days the pillory, stocks and 'cage', were close to the conduit. The punishments sound horrific and in complete contrast to the quiet gentility of this Greek figure. The water nymph, or naiad, was moved to Springfield in 1814. Except for the gentleman with the dark rimmed glasses, who seems more interested in the antics of the little girl at the front, the people gathered here at Oaklands Park Museum seem spellbound by the naiad's beauty. The nymph was acquired by the Chelmsford Society, and was presented to the museum in October 1964. The naiad now stands in one corner of the foyer of the Shire Hall where she is protected from the elements. Made, as she is, from Coade stone, a kind of concrete, she was beginning to show the ravages of time.

Shopping spree

T his busy traffic scene recorded at the junction of High Street and Springfield Road looks like an extract from a traffic policeman's training manual! A lot of effort appears to have been put into the job of making the confluence of pedestrians and motorcars as confusing as possible. Notice the zebra crossing on the right of the picture with shoppers, a cyclist and a car upon it simultaneously. The planners throughout Britain, let alone Chelmsford, were struggling to get to grips with the growing number of motors on our roads in the 1960s. And no wonder, for between 1953 and 1963 the number of cars in the country had risen from one car for every twenty-four people to one for every seven. Pedestrian crossings marked out by studs and yellow beacons were introduced in 1934; the first beacons were made of glass and made a wonderful target for little boys with stones, so the glass beacons were replaced by painted aluminium globes. Crossings got their stripes in 1951, and the beacons became plastic and began to wink in 1952. The 1934 Road Traffic Act had brought in the speed limit of 30mph in built up areas and made driving tests compulsory for new drivers, but even by the 1960s it was an uphill struggle to contain the toll of death and destruction on the roads.

Below: A mum proudly pushes her baby along Moulsham Street sometime in the 1950s accompanied perhaps by her older son. Coach-built prams like the one here are seldom seen nowadays and babies instead of having the supreme comfort of being wheeled around in such style are reduced to being pushed around at exhaust pipe level in fold-up buggies. Of course these were the days when shopping was something you did perhaps every day at the local shop and when you could safely leave a pram outside a shop and be confident that the pram and child would be there when you returned with your purchases. Today shopping tends to be more of a major expedition to an out-of-town supermarket which requires a bus or a car journey and a cumbersome pram is entirely unsuitable for this. The Windmill Inn pictured here with the original sash windows was demolished during the recent development of the Ring Road, but it was long a familiar feature of the town centre scene. Its front door opened into Moulsham Street but the back entrance to it was in Baddow Road opposite the Regent Theatre; its stabling, outbuildings and yard were situated on the way to Baddow Lane. The sign on the roofline advertises a car park - we can be sure that it wasn't crowded at this time. How many town centre scenes today could boast such an absence of litter?

Bottom: The absence of other pedestrians suggests that the picture was probably taken on a Sunday, but we know for certain at least, that the image dates from 1968. Several well-known retail names are visible in the photograph, including Millets the national chain famous for outdoor clothing and equipment and J H Clarkes the bookshop with its slogan - *My Books, My Good Companions.*
A solitary window-shopper was attracted by something in the music shop as he made his way along New London Road. The mature, if not elderly, gent had grown up in the era when families made their own entertainment with the aid of a piano bought in a specialist shop such as this. Contrast this with the era depicted here. The swinging sixties were well underway when this scene was captured; only a year earlier, in 1967, 2,500 young people were prosecuted for drugs related offences. The contraceptive pill became widely available in the mid 1960s, soon after The Beatles were awarded the MBE by Harold Wilson's Labour government in 1964. Apart from our male window shopper, the only other sign of life is represented by the Ford Anglia saloon disappearing down the street to the right. Anglias, with their unique slanted rear window were the cheap-and-cheerful transport of the masses in the 1960s and well into the 1970s.

Above: Tindal Square photographed from Tindal Street is extraordinarily quiet even for 1930. One can make a guess that the picture was taken early in the morning before many horses had chance to make use of the horse trough in the centre of the picture and leave their mark on the road! The single bicycle parked against the kerb has almost certainly not been chained up - something which would be decidedly unwise today: but people were very much more trusting in those far off days. And it is quite possible that the two motor vehicles in view were not locked either - the car on the right hand side notably features a 'Dicky' seat, an extra seat accessed by opening the boot in which two additional passengers could be accommodated and travel in the fresh air. One interesting feature on the skyline is what appears to be a greenhouse but is in fact Fred Spalding's studio. Below the studio is Harrison & Son selling ironmongery, tools and cutlery whilst to the right is Debnam's tobacconists established in 1860. Today both premises are estate agents. Next door, to the right, Bellamy's chemists has been replaced by the Bristol & West whilst the smaller building the right of Bellamy's is now an employment agency.

Right: A bustling scene in Tindal Street and Square as it was in the late 1940s. The distinctive tower of the cathedral with its clock face bears a flagpole on this picture and the flag is gently unfurling in the breeze. On the extreme left the Corn Exchange can be seen, this was built in 1831 and was the scene of a great deal of commercial activity for many years, as farmers from the surrounding countryside would come with samples of their harvest and try to get a good price for their grain. It was a place, no doubt, where farmers could commiserate with each other about the fluctuating fortunes of the farming industry, as well as where the merits and otherwise of new methods and technological innovations purporting to assist the farmer were hotly debated. Sadly this fine building was demolished in 1969. Across the street are the premises of R Walters wines and spirits, perhaps also the haunt of many a farmer on market days. Cobbe & Winam and Godfrey's Tents and Ropemakers as well as Bellamy's Chemist shops are on the far side of the square. Today's trend towards pedestrian precincts is restoring the balance in favour of shoppers on foot once more. The bus on the extreme right is a reminder that the first steam buses were made in Moulsham Street by a firm which later went on to become the National Bus Company.

Essex Libraries

In the 1950s there were such things as lines of parked cars. How different our town centres look today. With pedestrianised areas, multi storey car parks and traffic restrictions it is a whole new scene. The learner driver was heading away from the corner of Tindal Street and London Road, leaving behind JH Clarke's printers. Even though the road looked busy, it was an easier job for a new driver than it now is. He did not have to worry about mini roundabouts, one way systems or multi lane highways. It was a straightforward mirror, signal, manoeuvre and thank you very much for a full licence. The learner did have to use hand signals, something that the modern driver

does not require. He had to stick an arm out of the window and display that strange circular movement that meant a left turn was coming up. Many cars still had semaphore style indicators. A little, dimly illuminated flag popped out at the side of the vehicle. That was the technology of the day. Flashing indicators, known as winkers, were reserved for newer and smarter models. Some of the big high street names of half a century ago have survived the changes. Halfords and Marks and Spencer are still with us, but other shops have felt the draught of progress. They are just a memory of the days when you parked at the side of the road and popped into the shop.

High Chelmer - shopping for the past, present and future

Shopping can be a pleasure or a chore. It is not too long ago that housewives would take the bus into the centre of Chelmsford to do their weekly shopping armed with shopping bags and dragging unwilling small children along with them to load up with the necessities of life whilst carrying their heavy loads around a wide area. How many of us recall seeing such heavily burdened women heroically struggling through the wet streets or perhaps stopping for a moment to rest their heavy bags on the ground to pass the time of day with a friend; inevitably bored youngsters held their mothers' hands quietly for a few minutes before

beginning that incessant tugging which said unmistakably 'can we go home now?' And we were those children.

Yet for all our boredom and desire to get back to a warm fire or play with our friends, the memory of going shopping with mother lingers in the mind - and indeed it was not all boredom. The reward for being dragged around all the shops we did not want to go in might have been to be taken to look in a toy shop and stand in front of the window making out our personal wish list of toys or games we would dearly love to see in our

Above: The newspaper report on the planning meeting. Below: High Chelmer site c1949 - home of the Cattlemarket and Corn Exchange building.

Christmas stockings or receive as a birthday gift. Usually the thing we craved most was something that we would never actually own: that hugely expensive walking, talking doll or a Meccano set so huge we believed that if only we possessed it we could build a full size replica of the Forth Bridge over the River Chelmer - or construct cranes and earth movers with which we could rebuild the whole of Chelmsford.

In the end of course we didn't need to have a giant Meccano set, or even do the job ourselves. Others would come along and make drastic changes according to their vision of what the town needed and not to our childish dreams of a modern town centre roughly similar to something that Dan Dare, Pilot of the Future would have instantly recognised and felt at home in.

Chelmsford has been the shopping centre of mid-Essex for 800 years since King John first granted it a licence to hold a weekly market. During the Middle Ages retail premises developed along Moulsham Street and Baddow Road, but later, as the town expanded, the High Street became the main shopping area.

With greater pressure on space within the town centre the livestock market eventually relocated to Boreham. The weekly market was retained however and eventually refurbished to become an under-cover retail market now open five days a week.

Demand for retailing outlets in the middle of the town would eventually result in a modern shopping

Above: *Press releases on the modernisation of the shopping centre.*

centre - High Chelmer - built in the early 1970s and modernised in 1985, providing over 80 additional shops. Pedestrianisation of the High Street followed in the early 1990s and a second centre, The Meadows, was built in 1992 at the south end of the High Street. A town-wide CCTV system costing £600,000 was introduced soon after. This, together with attractive seating and planted areas and over 8,000 car parking spaces provides a safe, clean shopping environment for customers and tourists alike.

Today the traditional market, historic Moulsham Street, High Street and Chelmsford's two modern shopping centres provide a wealth of shopping opportunities from department stores to small specialist shops, all within walking distance of one another.

Since being redeveloped in the mid 1980s High Chelmer, the town's largest shopping centre, has been transformed. Today the centre boasts a distinctive polycarbonate-barrelled roof providing both lighting and ventilation. More than £200,000 was invested in providing new manual and automatic doors and special high absorbency matting. In 1997 several units were extended to keep pace with retail trends of the day. High Chelmer enjoys a patronage of in excess of seven million customers per year, counted by infra-red beams strategically located at each of the three mall entrances.

High Chelmer is managed by LaSalle Investment Management for the British Coal Pension Fund. In 1999, LaSalle merged with Jones Lang Wooton to become one of the world's leading fully integrated real estate services and investment management firms with over 680 million square feet of office, retail and industrial space and $21.5 billion (£13.5 billion) of assets under management. The merged company operates in 97 key markets in 33 countries on five continents.

ESSEX CHRONICLE
220th YEAR · FRIDAY, APRIL 6, 1984 · PRICE 20p

£2m facelift for precinct

A £2 MILLION facelift should give Chelmsford one of the lightest, brightest and most cheerful shopping centres in the south east by next year.

...and Exchange Way covered

28th October 1983

ESSEX CHRONICLE
FRIDAY, OCTOBER 28, 1983 · PRICE 20p

FACELIFT PLAN FOR PRECINCT

by Liam McAuliffe and Steve Clow

The story of High Chelmer goes back to the late 1950s and the beginning of the 1960s when the borough and county councils worked out a master plan for Chelmsford which would take the town into the 1980s and beyond. The town population was expected to double in those 20 years: a pedestrianised central shopping area was planned comprising High Street, Lower Moulsham Street, Friars Place with an extension over the area between Tindal Street and the River Can. The two secondary shopping areas near the centre of Upper Moulsham Street and the junction of Duke Street/Bromfield Road would be retained but their growth would be restricted and eventually also become pedestrian precincts. The plan was put on public display at the meeting of the County Council on the 2nd of July 1963.

Two years later when the huge bundle of plans for reshaping the heart of Chelmsford went to the Minister of Housing it carried with it the approval of nearly every trader in the town. Initially nearly 40 objections had been received from the Chelmsford Chamber of Commerce and traders objecting the plans themselves of the associated compulsory purchases. But at a three day public enquiry the objections dwindled to a handful as one by one the traders and the Chamber of Commerce withdrew their objections.

Right and below: *High Chelmer main malls prior to the 1985 refurbishment.*

The objectors' chief target was the proposed new social hall to replace the Corn Exchange, particularly the fact that it would be on the first floor and not be large enough.

The plans themselves were for a new shopping centre with 135 shops, a multi storey car park, riverside flats, offices and a new stall market with a service road. At the enquiry counsel for the local and county councils described the area as it stood as 'having a thoroughly ramshackle air... it looks like some of the less attractive parts of Paris before the fall of the Bastille' adding for good measure that parts of the street pattern were fit only for horse drawn vehicles.

The proposal would mean the replacement of 30,000 sq ft of shopping space with 315,000 sq ft of shops.

With objectors appeased matters could move forward. Five years after the public enquiry, in 1971, the multi-million pound redevelopment of Chelmsford town centre - CDA 15 as it was known - was nearing completion and in the process becoming the greatest change the town had ever seen. Residents of Chelmsford spent quite some time during the years of construction watching builders at work and peering with curiosity, and sometimes with apprehension, over what the finished product might look like. Would the final result be an asset to the town or be just another soulless brick construction which would lead to Chelmsford looking just like every other town in the country? Opinions were divided with voices heard in the pubs and cafés exchanging views, some, the optimists, predicting a grand future for the new centre whilst the more pessimistic happily predicted gloom and

The original plans were for a shopping centre with 135 units, a car park, flats, offices and a market

doom, sky high rates and even higher rents to pay for the development.

In September 1970 the first stage of the two phase plan to change the heart of Chelmsford had been completed with the opening of the multi storey car park. The High Chelmer Shopping Centre was finally completed in October 1973 when the final shop opened that month. In less than five years workmen had completely erased the patchwork quilt of warehouses sheds and shacks which had long occupied the area and built what one commentator described as 'a shopping Las Vegas' on the bones of the old market town.

The CDA 15 development was undertaken by Chelmsford

Above: *High Chelmer Shopping Centre c1997, just prior to extension works to several retail units.*

Borough Council in partnership with Ravenseft Properties, a development which would satisfy the pent up demand in the town for extensive shopping facilities and undercover shopping and car parks. The design idea of CDA 15 was to make sure that the architecture would stand on its own feet and be independent of any existing design in the town - although the council did stipulate that it must be a good neighbour to the rest of the town by being on a scale, proportion and character appropriate to a county town. By that the council meant that it wanted the design of the buildings to be kept simple and use traditional materials rather than be monumental or elaborate and use modern materials such as stainless steel and coloured glass. The final stage of building was seriously disrupted in 1972 when building workers went on strike for more pay: the men were claiming a minimum rate of £30 for a 35 hour week, improved annual holidays and cost of living increases: how little £30 seems today and how easily we have forgotten the impact of inflation in those days, already in double figures and soon to soar to almost 30 per cent a year.

Store owners who had once passed though Chelmsford as if it had been a trading desert and quickly moved on to Southend, Basildon and Colchester were now queuing up to find a place there. Overnight it seemed Chelmsford had become a boom town where developers were keen to get in to a shopping centre where millions of pounds were passing through cash registers in air conditioned stores. A new sense of Chelmsford's importance in the world began to pervade the town. Residents now begin to walk the streets with a spring in their step as Chelmsford seemed to shrug off its sleepy market town image and embrace the excitement engendered by the new. The new shopping centre and related developments seemed to infuse Chelmsford with an increased zest for life and in the wake of rebuilding, the energy of the town was redoubled with new businesses and new residents flocking to the town in droves all contributing to making Chelmsford buzz with a level of activity and purpose it had not seen for a century.

The future seemed bright, but the reality would not be quite as perfect as developers had hoped. In the nature of things, what was once new eventually becomes old. A decade later the site was beginning to lose its lustre. Less than ten years after its opening, Central Square was being described as drab and uninteresting whilst vandals had made nightly visits to the area. A two million pound scheme to revitalise the centre was drawn up by the joint owners CIN Properties Ltd representing the National Coal Board Pension Fund and the borough council.

The £2 million face lift gave Chelmsford one of the lightest, brightest and most cheerful shopping centres in the county at the time.

Above: *High Chelmer Shopping Centre today.*

Plans for the overhaul included sealing off the precinct outside shopping hours to deter vandalism. The new style shopping centre would be completely re-roofed, re-floored, re-furbished and generally brightened up to provide much more daylight. A major feature would be an open plan cafeteria in the central square, set a few inches below the rest of the centre and partitioned off from shoppers by low-level reinforced glass. The planned café replaced original proposals for a pyramid-shaped centrepiece with a mirror-finished surround supported by four pillars under which several kiosks such as flower and sweet sellers would be positioned. Work on the improvements began in June 1984 and would take 12 months to complete, including an eight week stoppage over Christmas to avoid inconveniencing shoppers.

One fear at the time was that local ratepayers would have to contribute an excessive amount to the scheme, though rumours that the council's share of the cost would amount to over half a million pounds were denied by the council, since rent received from tenants at that time amounted to £625,000. This did not seem an insuperable problem, moreover shop rents would increase to reflect the improved facilities being provided to them.

Today the High Chelmer Shopping Centre has 83 fully occupied shop units and provides a convenient, modern under-cover shopping experience handy for the town's car parks. Housewives doing their shopping no longer have to trudge through wet streets or queue for buses lugging their heavy bags. The range and quality of goods on sale has increased remarkably over the passing years - as have prices, up ten fold or more since the time High Chelmer was built. The buildings of our childhood may have disappeared forever to be

replaced by modern, efficient, warm, clean and tidy edifices but some things never change: there are still those small boys and girls clinging to their mothers' hands; and whilst they perform the time-honoured tugging routine perhaps they too are indulging themselves with dreams of their futures in Chelmsford.

As the new millennium dawns in the County town of Essex, the High Street is once again set to adapt to the changing regional, national and indeed global retail trends. High Chelmer will also evolve in order to satisfy the desires and aspirations of its principle customers in order to maintain its position as the retail heart of the town centre.

Left and below: *The entrance to High Chelmer today.*

Making a living

A picture dating back to the time when most of our domestic and commercial gas was produced from coal - days long gone now. The old gas works were built only a few hundred yards away from Chelmsford town centre near the Chelmer and Blackwater Canal by Navigation Road. This was to ensure easy access to supplies of coal which was brought to the site by canal barge. These were the days when miners were confident of having a secure job for the whole of their lifetime, coal seams were sufficient for many years to come and the country's need for it seemingly endless. How different things look today, with nuclear power and the interest in renewable sources of energy. The works were demolished in the 1960s when North Sea gas came on stream. The North Sea has yielded plentiful supplies of both oil and gas since the early 1970s and has contributed enormously to the country's wealth. All gas appliances had to be modified so as to be able to burn the natural fuel. We are all familiar with the distinctive smell alerting us to the presence of gas in the air and although the smell is not pleasant it does warn us not to strike matches or have other naked flames in the vicinity; naturally occurring gas is odourless and the 'gas smell' had to be added so that any leaks were obvious to consumers.

Below: The Nash family occupied Broomfield Court, which can be seen in the trees, behind and to the left of the hospital. It was built in 1904 for Mrs Louisa Radcliffe. The entrance and stairs are clad in oak and chestnut panelling. Each of the two families, in their turn, planted the trees in the beautiful grounds, which many patients coming to the hospital benefited. Louisa Radcliffe planted 'Atlas Atlantica' the blue grey cedar, 'Liriodendron tulipifera' the tulip tree. She planted copper beaches and limes, and the wonderfully named 'Gingo Baloba' from China, as well as a Maiden Hair tree with its fan-shaped leaves. When Broomfield first opened it was the only centre for thoracic surgery and tuberculosis in Essex. It was carefully designed so that all bedrooms faced south and had their own balconies. Bedrooms were built as single or two-bedded accommodation. Every day patients were wheeled out onto the balconies covered in red blankets so that they could get the benefit of the fresh air and sunshine. When this three-storey sanatorium was opened in 1940, it cost a quarter of a million pounds, excluding equipment. The hospital opened at the outset of war and this in itself brought about a sense of comradeship that had a very special character of its own. Despite the tension and pressure of the times morale was sustained, a monthly magazine was produced containing jokes, poetry and anecdotes written by hospital staff and patients. They called their periodical the 'Fairy Ann'! This building, deliberately planned to be light and airy, presented many headaches for the staff responsible for the 'blackout' of wartime. Screens were lifted into place every night to satisfy the regulations, and removed the following day for the benefit of the patients.

Bottom: This photograph of the livestock market in Market Street was taken as long ago as 1910. Animals bought at the market were driven down Market Street, through Tindal Square, along Threadneedle Street and New Street to arrive at the railway goods yard for loading onto cattle trucks. What would today's motorists make of herds of animals being driven through the centre of Chelmsford, we wonder. From the direction of travel we can infer that the small herd of cattle pictured in the centre this scene is on its way to be sold rather than on its way to the slaughterhouse. On the right is Joslins Agricultural Engineers with its display of ploughs set out on the pavement in front of their premises ready to attract the attention of farmers suddenly finding themselves in possession of a pocketful of cash after selling their animals. At the time this picture was taken the horse was still the power source of choice for most farmers to plough their fields although steam powered traction engines had been in use for many years in competition with them. Who could have guessed then that within a single generation the horse would have virtually disappeared to be replaced by the diesel-driven tractor?

Below: Little lads used to chase fire engines on their bikes. As the bells on the appliances rang out, so a convoy of boys appeared as if by magic. This appliance had been tracked to a house fire on Wood Street. Chelmsford has a particular place in the history of the fire service. The earliest drawing of a fire fighting appliance is one of the machines invented in 1802 by a local man, William Janes. Insurance companies usually ran the earliest brigades. They were anxious to protect properties they had insured. Accidental fires became larger and more frequent during the growth of activity in the industrial revolution. Some unscrupulous owners saw arson as a simple way to make a profit. Essex and Suffolk Fire Insurance established its fire brigade in 1802. Firemen were paid five shillings (25p) for each fire they attended. Every fireman had an iron plaque on his house so that people could call to give the alarm. A superintendent was appointed at the princely sum of 30 shillings (£1.50) per week. His wage included rent free accommodation, but, in return, he was also expected to keep the fire station in Market Road clean and tidy, run the gas engine, flush the sewers in Springfield and help run the market. The town council took over the running of the fire brigades at the beginning of the 20th century. The first appliances were horse drawn. Even as late as 1920 the engine was towed by a tractor. A second-hand motor car was converted for use in 1924: it was not until a few years later that dedicated appliances were introduced.

Right: Tired after a hard day's work at either Hoffmann's Manufacturing Company, which is to the right through the tunnel, or at Marconi's radio factory, which is to the left through the tunnel in around 1950. Hoffmann's roller bearing factory was the first of its kind in the country, as Marconi's was the world's first radio factory. They employed so many workers that they had to agree to stagger the start, finish and lunch times. Here the workers are cycling home to a welcome cup of tea no doubt, but they may well have had to sweeten it with saccharin, as the rationing of sugar and one or two other items had not ended altogether. Their tea would not be in tea bags, and care would be taken to strain the tea whilst poring it, as the educational films screened during the war taught them. Who could forget the lady who went through the process of making a cup of tea as if she were talking to aliens from another world? It always brought laughter from the audience between the 'A' film and the 'B' supporting film. The bicycle has changed very little in basic design over the years, save perhaps for its height and handle bar shape. These riders sit up proudly as they move down the road in stately procession. The man in the centre foreground had better watch out for the 'Bobby' on his beat, as all bicycles should have an audible warning device. In other words - he has no bell on his bike. During the war both factories were prime targets for attack by the Luftwaffe, but on 19th December 1944 Hoffmann's received a direct hit from a V-2 rocket. Thirty-nine people died and 138 injured, of which forty-seven were serious injuries. Chelmsford was blitzed several times, but the people and their factories continued to work towards the final victory.

The SAFEST BRAKES in the WORLD

HYDRAULIC BRAKES

Essex Libraries

have felt quite so comfortable in 1697, when the Poor Act was passed requiring them, and the members of their family, to be identified by a badge to be sown 'upon the shoulder of the right sleeve of the uppermost garment - in an open and visible manner'. It had to be either red or blue, bearing the letters 'CP'. 'C' for Chelmsford, followed by the letter 'P' for 'pauper'. If they did not comply with this instruction, they were refused relief for themselves, their wives and children. Ratepayers became responsible for the housing of the poor. The problems grew as Chelmsford attracted settlers and this requirement of identification of paupers was necessary for the parish's legal poor to be identified. Because of this Chelmsford introduced the measures 13 years before the Act became law.

Swayn's Barn in Springfield was left, by William Davey in 1520, to the parish to provide sufficient revenue to provide fuel for the poor at Christmas. The barn became unsafe and eventually was demolished and the ground was sold to the adjoining landowner. The money was used to rebuild old church almshouses, 'making two tenements there to answer to the value of the rent of the Springfield barn'. Poorhouses were also provided, and were not always the unpleasant places they are often thought to be, they were not designed for punishment, that was the job of the House of Correction, but were a sensible way of offering employment to ease the burden of their cost.

on. An attendant filled the tank and wiped the windscreen. He offered to top up the oil and water. You drove away having received decent service. Compare that with doing it all yourself and having to go inside to the till. There you are lucky to get a civil word as an assistant takes the credit card, swipes it and hands you a receipt. The whole transaction can take place in complete silence. The cars in view have a special British feel about them. The Triumph Vitesse and Herald were part of a proud industry. Who can fail to long for the days when the 'rag top' Morris Minor 1000 bowled along our streets? Now it is all models from the Continent and the Far East, with exotic names like Corolla, Laguna and Punto. You knew where you were with a Riley Elf or Hillman Imp. They were nippy little cars with names that told you exactly what they were like. Our proud Rover and Landrover companies have been swallowed up and only keep their names as a pretence of British ownership. The London Road garage is on the site once occupied by Coleman and Morton. The company made ploughs, harrows and other farming equipment. The first steam traction engine to be seen in Chelmsford visited here in 1856. The Boydell traction engine clanked its way for nine hours before arriving here. It then went off, puffing clouds of billowing smoke, to the plough trials at Writtle.

Essex Libraries

Members at a meeting of the full Chelmsford Borough Council pause for the camera on 9 November, 1947. On the walls, behind the solemn faces of councillors seated at the curved formation of solid wooden tables, pictures of former Mayors of the Borough may be seen. At the centre of the table at the rear stands Ald Arthur Walter who only two days before this had been elected to serve another year as Mayor. The custom of giving the annual Mayoral dinner was continuing, but this year there was an additional problem with it as, in order to comply with a new Ministry of Food order, numbers of guests had to be reduced to 100. There had been a threat of a bus strike if police didn't give approval for a new traffic plan for Chelmsford, involving the prohibition of parking in many town centre streets. Not all news was gloomy however. Later that month a radio announcement informed the nation that Princess Elizabeth was to marry a man who 'many will know so well as Lieutenant Philip Mountbatten, Royal Navy'. Advertisers for Bournville Cocoa were assuring everybody that 'happy families have the cocoa habit' and 'a little Bovril goes down well'. We do not know whether any of this advice was followed in the royal household.

Taking the tube

The world of science is a mysterious one to those of us without a technical background. And yet we live in an age of applied science with the twentieth century being dubbed by some as the start of a whole new era: the Electronic Age.

Perhaps a new title for present times is appropriate: the last hundred years or so have seen changes which would have seemed like magic to our forebears: our ancestors could only dream of radio, television and satellites. And Chelmsford has been at the centre of many of these epoch making changes.

Marconi Applied Technologies, based in Waterhouse Lane, designs and supplies microwave/radio frequency power and imaging components for markets such as communications, medicine, science, space and radar.

The business was established over fifty years ago as the English Electric Valve Company. The company has since then developed world-leading expertise in vacuum tube and high performance imaging technologies.

EEV, the forerunner of Marconi Applied Technologies, itself began life as the Phoenix Dynamo Company in March 1947 but soon changed its name to the English Electric Valve Company and retained that name until 1988 when it would briefly become EEV Ltd.

The firm had long associations with Marconi. A vacuum laboratory had been established by Marconi's Wireless Telegraph Company Ltd in 1929 to develop vacuum tubes. The laboratory was then sited in a corner of the New Street, Chelmsford factory. The laboratory was nothing more than a single room outfitted with a diffusion pump, a spot welder, a hydrogen furnace and a desk. The laboratory grew slowly during the 1930s, and in 1939 it moved to new buildings at Great Baddow.

On the outbreak of war in 1939 the laboratories at Great Baddow were virtually taken over: in the early 1940s the Air Ministry and the Admiralty absorbed the whole team working there.

Below: *Waterhouse Lane, Chelmsford.*
Bottom: *The original farm and wartime buildings of EEV's Waterhouse Lane site.*

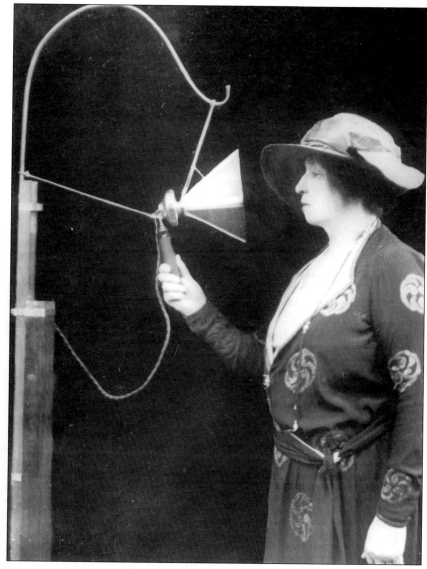

Between the end of the war and 1947 demand for valves shrank and the labour force at Waterhouse Lane fell to 150 by the time English Electric Valve Ltd was formally created. Waterhouse Lane would remain as the company's base from then on.

A painting made in 1874 (previous page) shows Waterhouse Lane winding its way towards Rainsford Road. In the foreground of the painting is a small wooden footbridge, replaced in 1922, over the River Can. A windmill on the site was later replaced by Mill House whilst a Georgian farmhouse was used by Marconi as a hostel for workers before eventually becoming a chemical laboratory for EEV. Two farmsteads also graced the site: Greater Waterhouse and Little Waterhouse. By 1934 however the farmhouse and land had been sold off, some of the land being bought by Marconi for a sports ground.

When the valve factory arrived in 1942 most of the farm buildings were still standing and were thought to be useful camouflage against air attack.

The development of efficient radar systems was a priority in the early days of the war and was based on two types. One was the ASDIC anti-submarine device, the other was the modified, Air Ministry designed, ASV (Air to Surface Vessel) to provide aircraft warning for small shipping. In addition a crash programme for a small radar set suitable for the detection of surface vessels was instituted. These developments helped reduce shipping losses but the modified ASV was unwieldy because the antenna system was fixed and so vessels had to turn in order to get a bearing.

Work developing radar continued apace. In May 1942 the need to step up development and production of the UK's first high power magnetrons caused the vacuum laboratory at Great Baddow to be transferred to Waterhouse Lane in Chelmsford. 9,000 sq ft of space there was dedicated to the production in what had been a garage for Marconi vans. Production quickly increased from 20 per week to eventually reach 2,500 a month by 1945 turned out by the company's 450 workers.

Above: Madame Melba at the Extemporary Microphone used for her first broadcast in the UK in June 1920.
Right: Dr Serge M Aisenstein.

At that time Waterhouse Lane was still a narrow Essex country lane with high hedges on both sides petering out just as the road passed the EEV site. A gatehouse was erected in the early 1950s but it was much later before a perimeter fence was erected. Today the site, with one exception, is entirely covered by a modern purpose built factory, laboratory and office buildings. The exception is a 16th century barn which stands near the main entrance and has been preserved as a staff dining room. The name Waterhouse incidentally has its origins going back to the 14th century when the land was owned by one 'John atte Water'; a century later the land was recorded as being owned by 'le Waterhous'.

EEV came about as result of the nation-alisation of the Cable and Wireless company in 1947. Cable and Wireless

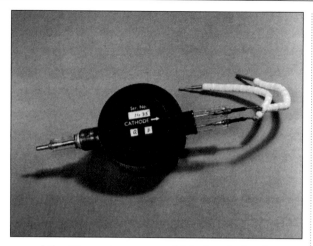

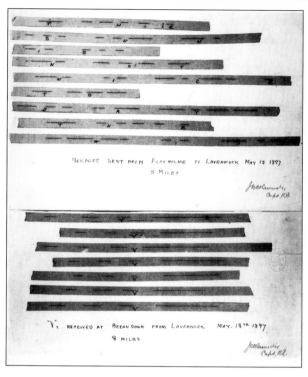

owned the Marconi company which then had to be sold. The English Electric company bought the shares.

The English Electric company had originated in 1918 with a merger of four businesses including the Phoenix Dynamo Manufacturing company. Phoenix was briefly resurrected in 1947 to serve as the trading name of the valve section at Waterhouse Lane but was very soon succeeded by the name of the English Electric Valve company or 'EEV'.

Once English Electric had acquired Marconi Wireless Telegraph the way was clear for the establishment of EEV. Pre-war agreements, suspended for the duration of the war, had prevented Marconi from manufacturing valves itself. The new company however was soon able to circumvent those earlier restrictions as well as develop other products.

In 1950 when the US airforce went home they left behind a lot of radar equipment which was acquired by southern air traffic control at Heathrow, for which EEV was commissioned to develop and supply new magnetrons. After they had been tested EEV was given a contract for 400. From then on government work would be about 25-30 per cent of turnover - deliberately kept at around that level to avoid being hit too badly by defence cuts.

A major problem in those early days was getting raw materials of adequate purity: molybdenum for example had to be imported from Austria; British glass was full of bubbles and seeds so the firm went to France for its glass, similarly high quality ceramics had to be imported from Germany.

Nor was the quality of raw materials the only problem encountered: the use of coal gas for glass working could introduce unwelcome impurities and so for certain processes hydrogen was used as an alternative. A more mysterious problem was that during the production of glass films blown by hand some operatives, all of whom were female, consistently or invariably produced a peculiar surface on the film, probably due to some unsuspected and undetected component in their exhaled breath - one particular

Above left: *A 1940s X-Band Magnetron.*
Above right: *Morse tape records of early wireless experiments from 1897.*
Below: *Waterhouse Farm, used in the early days as a chemical laboratory.*

girl for example would produce only yellow glass for two or three days each month and have to be taken off the work. As a result of a combination of problems over 50 per cent of every tube inspected was rejected.

The company's first orders for valves were from the Marconi Telegraph Company. Other orders soon followed and the customer list would grow to include the Admiralty, Ferannti, Decca, Edison Swann, GEC and many others.

In the 1950s it was realised that television was a growth industry. An agreement reached with the Radio Corporation America, RCA, allowed EEV to obtain an immediate lead over its competitors by realising the potential importance of the basic image orthicon under development by RCA. Eventually EEV became the major force in the manufacture of image orthicons and a leading manufacturer of other types of camera tubes. Thirty years after the introduction of the image orthicon the Encyclopaedia Britannica was still describing it as 'perhaps the most remarkable electronic device in existence'. Other UK and European camera tube manufacturers who had been active before the war persisted with the manufacture and development of tubes based on

pre-war concepts and only belatedly recognised the potential of the ultimate development of the basic image orthicon.

The two critically important features of the image orthicon were its sensitivity and stability, both lacking in its predecessors. Television outside broadcasts became a practical proposition despite widely varying light levels, and in the studio it could provide acceptable pictures at much lower light levels than those required previously - even, it was claimed, the light of a single candle was sufficient.

By 1954 it was clear that the market for image orthicons would continue to increase and a major expansion of production capacity was agreed. A new facility was erected on vacant land within the Waterhouse Lane site.

Above left and top: *Marconi Works in 1924 showing the masts and aerials for the BBC broadcast station.*
Below: *Marconi headquarters in the 1930s.*

The windowless building had three storeys and 37,000 sq ft of space. Operations were transferred to the new building in 1958. By 1982, when production of the image orthicons ended, more than 250,000 of them had been manufactured and assembled there.

By the close of the 1950s EEV had around 200 employees and a turnover of £2.5 million. EEV had begun its operations in a building occupying a mere 9,000 sq ft; by 1960 another nine buildings had been erected and occupied covering a quarter of a million sq ft. Products included magnetrons, klystrons, high power transmitting valves, vacuum capacitors, voltage stabilisers, hydrogen thyratons as well as image orthicons and other products.

During the 1960s further product developments took place, not least the Leddicon colour television camera tube and the pulse klystron, a final amplifier in an airport radar set - a development which was put to good use when BBC television proposed to switch from broadcasting on VHF to UHF wavelengths, requiring a

series of new transmitters. That development led to EEV becoming one of the world's largest suppliers of high power klystrons.

In 1968 when the English Electric Valve company was celebrating both its 21st birthday, and a turnover of £7 million, it was acquired by GEC and the company moved into a period of co-operation with another GEC subsidiary the Marconi-Osram Valve Company or M-OV. In 1963 M-OV equipment had been used to transmit signals to Telstar the world's first communications satellite and M-OV had become Europe's largest cathode ray tube manufacturer.

In 1977 EEV celebrated its 30th anniversary with a spectacular fete at Chelmsford for employees and their friends hosted by Rolf Harris. It was a good time to take stock: the Chelmsford site was around ten times larger than it had been in 1947 comprising some 400,000 sq ft and was set to grow to 600,000 sq ft three years later.

Above: *Celebrating the Queen's Award for Technology.*

EEV's annual turnover was close to £10 million and was one of the most impressive and experienced tube manufacturers in the world, and one of the largest. In the early days EEV had just three main customers the UK government, Decca and Marconi; 25 years later the whole range of power valves, microwave tubes and light conversion devices were sold on a world-wide basis to hundreds of customers. By 1972 about 40 per cent of turnover was for export plus a further 20 per cent in indirect exports comprising of EEV's contributions to exported radar systems, television transmitters and TV cameras.

Trading profits in the 1970s ranged from £1.1 million at the beginning of the decade to £5.1 million at its end. In 1978 sales were £23 million and by 1983 had risen to £44 million annually. By 1989 the firm was employing 2,500 and turnover had reached £80 million.

But there was a cloud on the horizon: The advocates of solid state technology had described tube makers as a 'bunch of boilermakers' to which EEV had replied confidently 'Quite right, but we make the best boilers in the business'. Whilst such confidence in the future of vacuum tubes was not misplaced the future however lay with solid state technology, something which EEV and Marconi would embrace with a vengeance combining all aspects of new and 'traditional' vacuum tube technology to produce amongst other products image intensifiers for military and civilian use as well as a host of other state of the art products such as liquid crystal display (LCD) systems with which to tempt clients.

Today Marconi Applied Technologies is a global supplier of equipment used in high power TV broadcasting, radiotherapy equipment, components for radar systems, power devices for laser eye-surgery and satellite up-link amplifiers used by TV outside broadcast vehicles as well as components for high energy particle accelerators such as the CERN project in Switzerland. Yet vacuum tubes still remain at the heart of the business - perhaps surprisingly there are still many things which the otherwise unstoppable micro chip cannot yet do so well!

Above: *Brazing an early Mercury Vapour Thyratron.*
Below: *Marconi Applied Technologies headquarters in Chlemsford.*

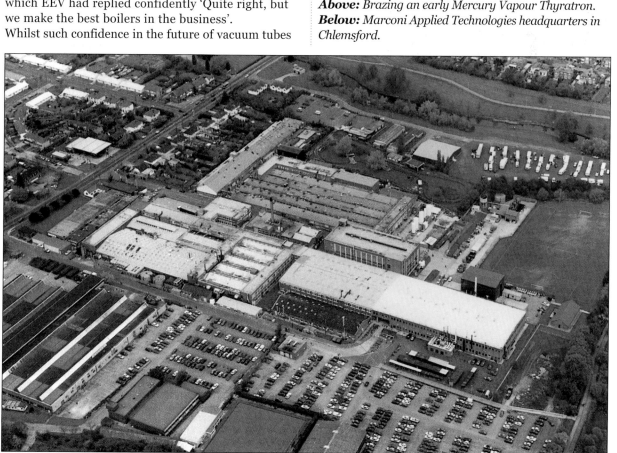

M&G - a history of innovation

Unit trusts - or 'mutual funds' - were conceived in the USA and made their first appearance in the UK in 1931. Chelmsford's famous M&G was the founder of the unit trust movement in the UK and its first manager was largely responsible for drafting the principles which went into the parliamentary Act governing unit trusts from 1939 until 1988 when the current Financial Services Act was passed.

The M&G company however has its origins much further back than 1931. In 1870 JG White, a construction engineer in the USA, founded a company called JG White Inc. JG White built subways and came to the UK around 1900 to extend that business operating from 9 Cloak Lane, London.

A second important character was George Booth, an intellectual born in 1877 and a member of the Alfred Booth shipping company family. In 1917 Lloyd George asked Booth to become a member of

the war cabinet as Munitions Minister. On one of George Booth's regular visits to the USA he met JG White.

After the war George Booth bought the UK subsidiary of JG White. The company built many well known buildings such as the Ritz and the Waldorf Hotel in London and also constructed many tramways throughout Britain.

Building such large public projects as tramways often meant local authorities having to raise money. To facilitate raising such loans George Booth established a subsidiary company of JG White's called Municipal and General Securities - the forerunner of M&G. Raising funds in this way was a common practice in the USA and something that JG White Inc had done years earlier.

M&G was the founder of the unit trust movement in the UK

Below: *Victoria House, as it was when the company purchased it.*

OFFICES TO LET

The background to all this activity was the Wall Street crash in 1929 and its parallel in London. The collapse of hectic speculation left many investors ruined and the survivors disillusioned. For the man in the street the principle of a 'collective investment vehicle' in those days was the 'investment trust' as it was and is still called; although this was not a trust but in fact a company; at the time there were many sound investment trusts - but also many other kinds with minimal regulation.

Using the Municipal and General ('M&G') part of the JG White business, and now renamed White-Drummond, George Booth was inspired by the 'mutual fund' concept pioneered in the USA which allowed investors to spread their risk over a range of companies. Adapting this concept for the UK M&G produced the First British Fixed Trust. The 'fixed' element meant that every time shares were sold more had to be bought from a fixed range of stocks. The new fund was launched on St George's Day, 23rd April, 1931.

George Booth recruited Ian Fairbairn, the third and most critical figure in M&G's genesis, to manage that first fund. Fairbairn's experience was only partly common to others of his station in the City: he was an Eton scholar, he had been in the Great War and had some political interests but he had also taken a degree at the LSE; he had profound opinions about the need for encouraging thrift in the small saver but wanted to encourage it in ways in which investors could directly benefit from economic growth. Fairbairn thought the First British Fixed Trust to be an important development in that direction. Ian Fairbairn's eventual claim to fame was that he became the father of the unit trust industry in Britain, the architect of M&G and guardian of the whole industry.

A Second British Fixed Trust followed the first in 1932, a Third appeared in 1933 and two more a little later. By then however the popularity of fixed trusts and the size of the funds made the 'Fixed' formula too rigid and by the mid 1930s the first Flexible Trust was launched, which was the beginning of modern fund managing.

The 1930s, until 1937, were a bullish period for the stock market and though the approach of war caused a decline in shares, the economy was still progressing well. Many more unit trusts were created during the period in imitation of M&G but not all of them set the same self imposed standards as Ian Fairbairn set for M&G. He lobbied for regulation of the industry and was rewarded in 1939

Above: An early leaflet issued by Municipal and General Securities.

with a section of the Prevention of Fraud (Investments) Act which regulated unit trusts.

In 1939 the second world war began and until the war's end there were no more issues of funds to raise capital through unit trusts.

The outbreak of war put a stop to reform and to most normal capital raising; it would not be until 1957 that capital controls were removed, and not until 1958 that the Investments Act was revised and unit trusts in their modern form could operate freely once more.

Rather sooner, after the war came a relaxation of some restrictions. In 1951 M&G, still with a mere 35 employees at its London offices, managed to put together the bulk of its pre-war funds into the M&G General Trust Fund. The M&G Thrift Plan began in 1954, the UK's first unit trust regular savings plan, in which one could invest just 5 shillings a week in unit trusts.

In 1959, following the lifting of wartime restrictions, Ian Fairbairn invited the merchant bankers Robert Benson Lonsdale (later to become Kleinwort Benson) to take a minority stake in M&G. His reasons were twofold: firstly to allow an injection of much needed capital for expansion; secondly, take-overs were in the air and the Kleinwort Benson deal allowed M&G to remain independent.

Two years later, in 1961, Fairbairn established the Esmée Fairbairn Charitable Trust (named after his wife who had been killed in a wartime air raid) with a 50.1% holding in the group as a bulwark against predators, though with a primary duty to finance education in investment.

In 1962 M&G started M&G Trust Assurance (which would become M&G Life Assurance) on the basis that one could then get tax relief on premiums paid into a Life Fund and, if one was a unit holder, one could therefore buy units more cheaply. Other new financial products soon followed.

M&G's Dividend Fund was launched in 1964, an income fund which was then a new concept and which was to become an important factor in M&G's development. Another famous product first sold in 1966 was the Family Bond, though the last of these has now long since matured. Endowment Bonds appeared in 1968 to take advantage of tax relief on lump sums until they matured.

By 1968, the company was employing nearly 200 people and a small contingent of M&G's securities and administration staff were moved from London to offices in Victoria House, New London Road, Chelmsford.

M&G's main competitor, Save & Prosper, had by that time become a giant of the unit trust industry having over 30% of the market. M&G was however, still the third largest company in the field after the National Group. One of the reasons for the static performance of M&G was its refusal to become involved in the 'block offer' side of the business in which units were issued at a

Above: Three early M&G advertisements.

Buying shares in companies in trouble involves some risk, but M&G's familiarity with companies made it well placed to assess risk and spot opportunities.

This fund would ultimately become one of M&G's largest funds and grow to over a billion pounds; in addition, it was the best performing fund, not simply in its sector, but covering all sectors for the first ten years of its existence.

1969 was also a notable year for another reason: the M&G name having by then become universally recognised, the unit trust management company was formally renamed M&G Securities Ltd having still been called the Municipal and General Securities Company Ltd until then.

Two years later a new policy began of investing in the international market starting with a Japan & General Fund. M&G became the first UK fund manager to specialise in that area.

fixed price, which M&G felt created a false feeling of scarcity which it believed was not something unit trusts were about.

The following year, 1969, was an important year for M&G because it launched its Recovery Fund, a fund which buys shares in companies which are out of favour or in difficulty.

Above: *The impressive entrance to M&G's premises at Victoria Road.*

Despite the stock market fall of 1973/74 M&G coped well: in 1974 it had launched Guaranteed Deposit Bonds, a deferred annuity and an immediate annuity, which gave yields of 11%, which was 1% above everyone else. Around two million pounds a day flowed into that fund preventing M&G from suffering in the way that many of its competitors did at that time.

Growth meant additional staff and in 1975 the company appointed its first real actuary.

In 1979, M&G's association with Kleinwort Benson continued, with Kleinwort Benson increasing its stake in the company to 37.4%. By 1986, Kleinwort Benson decided that M&G would do better if its shares were held by a wider audience so the 28 million shares in M&G which Kleinwort Benson owned were offered to the general public. The Kleinwort Benson sale left the Esmée Fairbairn Trust with 33% of shares, as the only major shareholder. The shares were offered at 270p; within ten years they would have tripled in value, those who bought them doing very well indeed.

By 1986 the combined staff in Chelmsford and London had risen to 380 and the company moved from Chelmsford's New London Road to M&G House in Victoria Road. This was a time of expansion, during which M&G established a quality service centre for customers. This meant that customers received personalised replies to queries and enabled them to have all their investment enquiries dealt with by telephone on a one-to-one basis.

1986 was memorable for passing longstanding rivals, Save & Prosper, to become the UK's largest unit trust group. The crash of October 1987, which was only the fourth month since 1926 when the market fell by over 20%, passed, in retrospect, with virtually no impact. M&G again led the industry when it launched PEPs at their outset in 1987, when the allowance was only £420 a year.

However, 12 years later M&G had over half a million PEP accounts and £4 billion in PEPs.

Innovation gathered pace - the first European Income fund (now European Blue Chip) was launched in 1989, followed by the largest ever investment trust launches in 1991 and 1992 to take advantage of a quirk in the PEP rules.

The start of M&G's fixed income leadership began in the early 1990s with the launch of The Corporate Bond Fund (followed by the first High Yield Corporate Bond Fund in the UK in 1998). To this day M&G remains the UK's biggest fixed income manager with over £35 billion under management. M&G also launched the UK's first no initial charge

Below: *M&G House.*
Bottom: *M&G's new Fairbairn House offices.*

PEP - Managed Income. But by the mid 90s the signs of the need for change were clear. M&G had always emphasised value and avoidance of fashion in share selections. However, the times had changed.

Following the retirement, in 1995, of Paddy Linaker (who joined in 1963) and David Morgan in 1997, a new management team was appointed. The new team was led by Chief Executive, Michael McLintock, who had joined M&G in late 1992. The need for change was understood. The fund range was updated, along with the investment process and a new look in marketing.

All these developments were reflected in Chelmsford, where staff had grown to over 700 and millions of pounds were invested in state-of-the-art technology, enabling M&G to enhance a quality service to nearly three quarters of a million customers.

In March 1999, the Prudential shocked the UK stock market with an audacious £1.9 billion bid to buy M&G. It would be money well spent.

Above: Some of the financial products offered by the company today.

One of the reasons for the high price, 10 per cent of M&G's £19 billion assets, was the need to gain the backing of the Esmée Fairbairn Trust, still a 33 per cent shareholder. The deal was a key step in the Prudential's drive to reinvent itself as a modern financial services player. The 'Pru' was already the UK's largest pension provider; after swooping on M&G it also became the biggest unit trust seller.

Unlike rivals which have chosen to launch their own stand-alone fund management business Prudential recognised it made more sense to acquire an already established brand - and Prudential has preserved M&G's historic identity rather than attempting a massive re-branding.

M&G is now the European investment management arm of the Prudential and the engine room behind the sale of mutual funds to the public.

At the beginning of this new millennium, M&G employs some 1,500 staff and is preparing to expand into Chelmsford's Fairbairn House in addition to its Victoria Road offices.

Brewing an enduring success

The Ridley family can be traced back to the tenth century English Royalty and to the rugged Scottish Borders county of Northumberland and the lush areas of Cumberland.

Notable personalities in the Ridley family are Bishop Nicholas Ridley, martyred for his faith during the reign of Queen Mary, Sir Thomas Ridley, Master of Eton School and Marke Ridley, physician to the Czar of Russia in 1595. In 1786, William Ridley set up as a tanner in the small town of Clare in Suffolk. He moved to Essex following his marriage to Maria, daughter of a mill owner in Hartford End. On the death of Maria's father, they took over the mill.

In 1814, Maria gave birth to Thomas Dixon Ridley and it is after him that T D Ridley & Sons is named. He took on his father's business, expanding the milling side. In 1841 he married Lydia Wells, who

Above: *Thomas Dixon Ridley.*
Right: *Nicholas Ridley - Executive Chairman.*
Below: *A South Eastern view of the brewery.*

came from a brewing family in Chelmsford. Within a year, Thomas Dixon had built his own brewery downstream from the mill.

The business expanded rapidly and by 1882 the year of Thomas Dixon's death, he had already established a chain of inns. In 1906, the business was formed into a 'limited company'.

The business has been passed down through succeeding generations and is still a family company. Today Nicholas Ridley, great great grandson of Thomas Dixon Ridley, is Executive Chairman.

From producing just two beers in the comparatively recent past, Ridleys has expanded to offer a comprehensive portfolio of seven cask conditioned ales to cater for all tastes. These include the award winning IPA and Rumpus which was only launched in 1996 but has already become one of the brewery's top three cask brands.

Last year the pub estate increased by 11 per cent and the brewery now own in

supermarkets including Sainsbury, Tesco and Waitrose.

The Ridleys name is promoted by a range of sponsorships - both national and local. For many years Ridleys sponsored Essex County Cricket Club. This deal included track suits, sweatshirts and 'T' Shirts worn by the players, as well as Player of the Month/Year awards and brought great awareness of the Ridley brand both nationally and in Essex. As part of a two year deal Ridleys sponsor Colchester United's new away kit which enabled them to promote their beers around the country, this market already accounts for one third of their sales.

Co-ordinated by Ridleys in association with BBC Essex, the Essex 'Sports Achievers Awards' recognise county sportsmen and women who have worked tirelessly behind the scenes and contributed to the success of a club, centre, team or

excess of 60 public houses, with more being added every year, new pub purchases will be situated further afield than the current locations in order to attract new drinkers and help expand the direct free trade.

As a long established independent brewer, Ridley's has the experience and expertise to produce bespoke beers quickly and efficiently and they produce a new event beer every six weeks to maintain drinkers' interest in cask ales.

Before 1992, it would have been rare to hear the brewery name outside the borders of Essex. Today, Ridleys has achieved national coverage for its ales through a comprehensive distributor network with pub groups like Burtonwood, Enterprise Inns, Pubmaster, J D Weatherspoon, Scottish Courage and Whitbred as well as national wholesalers, such as The Beer Seller, Matthew Clark Wholesale and Tavern Wholesaling.

Ridleys has ventured into the off licence trade with bottled brands now being stocked in major

Top left: Early morning malt delivery.
Top right: An 18th century cast iron Barrell.
hoist. ***Above right:*** *A range of Ridley's 500ml bottles.*

individual. The winners are chosen by a distinguished panel of judges. The awards culminate with a gala presentation dinner, which is broadcast live on BBC Essex. The three top winners in each category are invited with a guest to the dinner to enjoy a fun evening with Essex celebrities.

Ridleys is entitled to enter five competitors in the gruelling 26 mile London Marathon, as they hold a golden bond ticket. Competitions to find worthy runners are run in the East Anglian Daily Times.

Ridley's brewer, regularly hosts tastings in pubs and clubs up and down the country asking drinkers 'How well do you know your ales?' Complete with sampling notes and an array of beers, Philip explains not only why the beers are different but also the different brewing methods involved.

Organised by prior arrangement, the brewery offers an insight into the workings of a traditional tower brewery through its brewery tours. Visitors also enjoy the comforts of the brewery's hospitality suite, the Clock House, where they sample Ridleys' many top quality ales.

To enhance the environment and to make pubs more enjoyable places to visit, the brewery runs an annual competition to find the very best frontage and beer garden among all the Ridley outlets - both in tied and free houses. The pubs creating the most brightly coloured and imaginative flora and displays win garden centre vouchers. They also operate a Throne Room Challenge to promote

cleaner and more pleasant toilet facilities throughout the Ridley estate.

To encourage better cellar management, Ridleys run their annual cellar competition. Publicans are not only judged on the condition of their cellars, but the opportunity is used to supply up-to-date literature and hands-on training from its Cellar Services personnel.

As a major employer in Essex, Ridleys invests heavily in community initiatives, which allows the company to use its people, skills and resources to help regenerate communities. One such scheme is the Colchester Allotment Competition, run in association with Colchester Borough Council. The 'best allotment' is that which demonstrates the best combination of high standards of cultivation and horticulture, sensitivity to the environment, particularly in respect of chemical use, recycling and soil/water conservation, and safe orderly working practices.

Other initiatives include working with the rural Community Council of Essex to improve the quality

Above: *Some of Ridley's 'Event' beers.*
Below: *Ridley's Tower Brewery.*

more so than in the Brewhouse where Ridleys has taken care to retain the original brewing equipment including the mill and fermenting vessels.

During the winter months and especially in the weeks preceding Christmas, work in the Brewhouse starts well before dawn and finishes long after sunset. Ridleys insist on using only the best ingredients including the finest East Anglian Malt, the choicest Kentish hops and the Brewery's very own natural spring which provides a continuous source of the purest water.

Dating back to 1842 the mill is still in good working order thanks to continued maintenance over the years and the realisation that part are no longer easy to come by. Traditional brewing methods are still used and it is this which gives Ridleys ales the taste so appreciated by their customers and which will ensure that the company can continue to develop their range of traditional yet popular ales in the future.

of life in rural Essex by highlighting the need for new community services or equipment. In recent years, too, Ridleys has worked closely with Essex Wildlife Trust encouraging people to visit and learn more about areas of natural beauty.

Few would argue that Hartford End Brewery is one of the ten most picturesque breweries in the country. Surrounded by fields and nestling on the banks of the River Chelmer, the brewery's original source of power, the brewery tower dating from the mid 19th century makes an impressive sight from a distance and is a constant reminder of a life now long past.

Tradition and family heritage remain the focal point of all who work at Hartford End. Nowhere

Above: *An early delivery dray.*
Top: *An advertising campaign.*
Right: *Part of today's fleet.*

Bolingbroke & Wenley - shopping paradise

The face of shopping in Chelmsford has changed and evolved for centuries, from market stalls to shops and from shopping centres to superstores. What next we wonder? All of us however remember the shops of our youth and only need to shut our eyes to recall exactly what businesses traded in each street during the happy years of years of our childhood.

In April 2000, when the High Street store of Bolingbroke & Wenley Ltd closed its doors for the last time, a chapter in Chelmsford's commercial history came to an end - though the event was far from the end of Bolingbroke & Wenley.

The company came into being in 1967 through the merger of two of Chelmsford's longest-standing family firms which had traded next door to each other for decades.

The Wenley family had begun selling furniture in Baddow Road as long ago as 1845 when William Gilson Wenley a cabinet maker and his son, also William Gilson Wenley, opened a shop there. According to family tradition there was already a customer waiting for them on the doorstep as they first arrived to open for business: tradition also says that they had to wait two weeks for their next customer!

It was however William Gilson Wenley III who in 1895 would rent 73 High Street, occupying virtually the same site for the next one hundred and more years. Six years later the premises were bought and renovated

Left: A steam powered vehicle used for removals until 1922. Above: By late 1922 petrol engined vans and trailers were employed. Below: The High street in 1912.

bought number 75 High Street at auction and extended his store sideways. At the time of the auction the firm's main rival was JG Bond Ltd (now Debenhams) on the other side of the street. Although Bonds did not want the premises itself neither did its owners want George Bolingbroke to expand and were prepared to outbid him. In the end George used a butcher to bid for him by proxy. Believing that a butcher would attract flies and detract from the Bolingbroke side of the street Bonds left the butcher's bid unchallenged and George Bolingbroke acquired additional premises at a knock down price.

For twenty years the two businesses co-existed alongside one another between the High Street and London Road. Both businesses became limited companies in 1917 as Wenley Ltd and Bolingbroke & Sons Ltd.

The two firms were always forward looking: in 1921 Bolingbroke & Sons became the first Chelmsford store

Top left: Bolingbroke's premises.
Top right: The fire that occurred in 1947.
Above left: Wenley & Sons' premises on High Street.
Below: An early showroom display.

with a mortgage for £14,000, the money being put up by the Capital & Counties Bank now part of the Lloyds TSB bank group.

Almost twenty years earlier, in 1876, George John Bolingbroke, in partnership with his brother-in-law John Ling, had opened his store at number 74 High Street.

George Bolingbroke had a background in agriculture but had left home to serve an apprenticeship with Marshal & Snelgrove in London's Oxford Street in retailing, working his way up to be a buyer in the lace department. On leaving that firm Mr Snelgrove was so impressed with George's potential that he gave him a personal loan of £1,000 - a very large sum in those days to finance his own store. Such faith was well founded, the loan was repaid within five years.

The Wenleys sold furniture, carpets, wallpaper and timber; Bolingbroke & Ling had a drapery business which included dressmaking for funerals, a not unusual combination in Victorian England when mourning clothes would frequently be specially made for the bereaved.

John Ling retired in 1882 leaving George Bolingbroke as sole proprietor. Ten years later George

to have a visit from Father Christmas, whilst in 1923 Wenleys became the first shop in Chelmsford to install a lift.

One of the major events for both firms occurred in 1947 when a disastrous fire broke out. Flames were seen coming from Wenleys on the evening of 24th June. The flames soon spread to both properties. When the fire had been quelled nothing was left of either shop save for part of Wenleys facing London Road. Happily however much of Bolingbrokes' stock was rescued by a small group of volunteers led by thirty year old Wray Bolingbroke, the founder's grandson.

Restoration and rebuilding took over three years to complete but in the end both premises were much improved including Wenleys' top floor restaurant. Wenleys was also able to expand further with the purchase of the adjoining property belonging to the Conservative Association which was then turned into a carpet showroom.

In response to ever more demanding fire regulations the two firms co-operated with each other allowing passages to be made through the party walls between the shops. In 1965 Richard Wenley, the great great grandson of William Gilson Wenley, reportedly walked through one of these doors to ask Wray Bolingbroke if a merger might be considered.

The marriage between the two companies was completed in October 1967 and Bolingbroke & Wenley Ltd came into being. The shops were fully amalgamated in 1968 with a single trading area on the ground floor after knocking down an arcade which had been a feature of the original shops.

In that same period the construction of the Chelmer Shopping Centre in London Road allowed the firm to open up the rear of the shop to trading from London Road.

In the late 1980s the company realised that the future was in out of town stores and

established a new outlet in Springfield for the furnishings side of the business. That store opened in 1991 taking the furniture and carpet departments from the High Street.

In 1999 decisions were made which would change the face of the company forever. After much debate the family shareholders of the company decided to accept an exceptionally good offer from a property developer for the High Street site. It was a wrench for the family but a sound business decision.

At the same time family directors John Bolingbroke and Simon Watkins (of the Wenley family), prepared a business plan to buy out the out of town furnishing store from the existing shareholders. The bid was successful and the company could move forward with its plans to acquire the Sainsbury's Homebase store, significantly larger premises.

All things change but, as the familys' business baton is carried into the 21st century, six generations of the Wenley family and four generations of Bolingbrokes prove that fortunately not everything changes at the same pace.

*Above left: A 1980s display. **Above right:** The combined Bolingbroke & Wenley stores. In this view the two separate buildings can clearly be seen. **Below:** Bolingbroke & Wenley today.*

Educational excellence

Anglia Polytechnic University started out as a School of Art founded in 1858 by the Victorian art critic John Ruskin at premises in Sidney Street, Cambridge. Ruskin intended the new school 'to teach Sight and not to try to teach Art in relation to any particular trade'. The school was a success and expanded rapidly eventually moving in 1889 to the site on East Road where the Technical College had just been built. Today, East Road is still the address of APU's Cambridge Campus. The site which later became the Essex Campus of the University however opened in Chelmsford in 1893.

In 1904 Lord Rayleigh laid the foundation stone in Market Road for the first purpose-built educational establishment in Chelmsford. Frederick Chancellor, a notorious architect and also the town's first Mayor designed a building on Victoria Road South which is now part of the University's Chelmsford Central site. That building is today home to APU's Planning Department, part of the School of Design and Communication. In 1931 new buildings were erected on the Victoria Road South site. The Mid Essex Technical College & School of Art was established in Chelmsford on the Chelmsford Central Campus in 1935. In Cambridge, 1960 saw the Technical College and School of Art becoming the Cambridge College of Arts and Technology (CCAT).

The Mid Essex Technical College and the Brentwood College of Education, opened in 1962, merged in 1976 to form the Chelmer Institute of Higher Education. The former Brentwood College became APU's Brentwood site for the School of Education. In 1984 The Chelmer Institute became the Essex Institute of Higher Education and in 1989 CCAT and the Essex Institute became independent statutory corporations and merged to form Anglia Higher Education College. The new college was granted Polytechnic status in 1991 and only eight months later it was granted University status, becoming Anglia Polytechnic University.

Since that time APU has achieved national and international recognition as an institution noted for academic excellence and in the vanguard of a new generation of universities.

In 1992 the university acquired the Rivermead Campus site in Chelmsford which had previously been the Hoffman Pollard ball bearing factory. Two years later the Queen's Building was completed. It was APU's first new building on the campus, formally opened by Her Majesty Queen Elizabeth II in June 1995.

Around the same time the Rivermead Student Village was completed providing over 500 bed spaces on the campus.

Above: *A view of the School of Art in 1906.*
Below: *Chelmer Institute in the 1970s.*

In June 1996, the second new building, Rivermead Gate, was built. This state of the art building not only houses academic staff but provides student amenities, including a supermarket, bank, laundrette, book shop and medical centre incorporating a doctor's surgery and a pharmacy. It was officially opened in October 1998. More space for future expansion was gained in 1997 when six acres of land were acquired from Chelmsford Borough Council. That same year the University centralised its nurse teaching to Chelmsford, a process which necessitated the acquisition of Ashby House, at Rivermead, the redevelopment of the Central Campus buildings and the development of a staff transport system.

Great strides have been taken in developing teaching and research. By January 2000 another state of the art building, the Sawyers Building, was completed at Rivermead, accommodating the School of Education now relocated from the Old Brentwood Campus. This housed a further 750 students and 75 staff. Facilities include a sports

Above right: *Frederick Chancellor Building, Central Campus.* **Top:** *Part of the Central Campus in the late 1970s.*

hall, laboratories, specialist IT teaching areas and a 'Time Out' area for students and staff. This is the latest stage of achieving plans to create a modern environment conducive to teaching, learning and research as well as meeting the needs of students.

In the last year of the 20th century Peter Taylor Hall was completed at Cambridge whilst in Chelmsford

completion of the North Bridge connected the Rivermead Campus with the public space on the far side of the river.

Following an anticipated donation of £5 million from Sir Michael Ashcroft, APU now plans to build a new business and management centre on the Rivermead Campus to be known as the Ashcroft International Business School.

Today there are over 21,000 students at the University making it by far the largest provider of education in the region. Both the Cambridge and Chelmsford Campuses have received enormous investment in recent years to ensure students have access to the best learning environment.

Whilst students come to APU from all over the world, the University aims to be the local university of choice by meeting the needs of as many students and businesses as possible within the region. In Essex, more than seven of every 10 full-time students live within 45 minutes of the campus and APU is constantly striving to improve on this figure through a proactive programme of events, advertising and promotions.

The East of England Development Agency has defined clear economic objectives for the region to attract more inward investment and create greater opportunities. Today APU is as much a part of the local, national and global life as any multi-national company. APU contributes to the region's economy on an on-going basis by working with organisations from a vast cross-section of sectors and industries to prepare individuals for work and enhance their existing skills. APU offers research and teaching expertise to today's industrial and commercial leaders which in turn, through feedback, ensures that the services offered remain responsive, flexible and innovative. APU carries out research and developmental projects and aims to provide a growing number of market research, consultancy and education services for business and public authorities.

As a centre of excellence in learning and teaching, supported by high quality research, the University's central aim is to equip students for work, giving particular priority to skills required in the region, by providing education and professional development in new technologies, the environment, leisure, personal development, health and social care. It also plans to continue offering full support to specialist research units.

Teaching via video conferencing facilities promises to open up new learning opportunities. For example the feasibility of a scheme to teach nursing courses in India using this method is being investigated.

APU's Enterprise & Innovation Office promotes, supports and generates income for the University through developing a range of products and services such as customised degrees and training courses, management development, IT, research and seconding staff to other organisations.

The University has many objectives but if an overriding one could be identified it would be to ensure that every adult - irrespective of age, gender, physical ability or geographical location, has access to learning. It has already done much to fulfil that objective.

Top left: The Queen opens the Queen's Building with the then Chancellor and Vice-Chancellor of APU.
*Top right: The Queen, with Chairman of Governors, Alan Cherry, greets APU students. **Above left:** The welcome procession for the Queen in front of the Queen's Building. **Left:** The Rivermead Gate Building.*

The caring, sharing Co-op

The co-op movement frequently traces its history from the Rochdale Equitable Pioneers' Co-operative Society founded in 1844, although its forerunners can be traced back at least as far as the 17th century. The first co-operative in Chelmsford - a coal club - was formed in 1847. Then, in 1867, Chelmsford Star Co-operative Society was established by a small number of employees of the London Road Iron Works: it was their intention to become 'the Star of the County'. The first shop was opened in Tindal Street and despite the economic problems of the 1870s the Society prospered to such an extent that its members soon decided to build a new store in Moulsham Street on the site of the present day Quadrant. Opened in 1881 by the author of 'Tom Brown's School Days', Thomas Hughes, it was a magnificent building: the Society had indeed become 'the Star of the County'.

The Countess of Warwick, a leading advocate for the co-operative movement, opened an extension to the building in 1902. Year by year, the range of products increased. More shops were opened in other parts of Chelmsford and in the surrounding villages. The Society also acted as an agency for the Co-operative Building Society and the Insurance Society.

A Co-operative Women's Guild was established by the Society's membership in 1906 and an Education Committee, funded and elected by members was formed in 1925.

The promotion of co-operative principles was a key element of the Education Committee's work and, with the establishment of International Co-operative Day in 1923, it pursued its task vigorously. International Co-operative Day, held on the first Saturday in July, was a grand affair for the whole community. From then until the second world war up to a thousand children

Above left: *Notification of the intention to start a Co-operative Society on February 18th 1867.*
Above right: *A 1929 milk-float at Chelmsford Star Dairy.* **Below:** *The Moulsham Street store in 1902.*

1930s, Chelmsford Star helped to alleviate some of the harshest cases of poverty by providing families with boots, clothing and food parcels. Later when the Hunger Marchers passed through Chelmsford on their way to London it was Chelmsford Star that provided them with a meal and repaired their boots.

By the second world war Chelmsford Star had a shop in virtually every locality within the town and surrounding countryside. It had established its own abattoir, mobile shops, travel department, clothing store, funeral service and much more. It had also established a Co-operative Party Council in 1943 and the Education Committee had formed Youth and Children's Clubs.

Since its formation Chelmsford Star has supported the community; as early as 1883 when donations were needed for the Chelmsford Infirmary the membership regularly agreed to allocate part of their surplus to the hospital. Throughout its entire history the Society has sponsored many local organisations. That tradition has continued: in the 1970s the Society organised a series of annual 'It's A Knockout' competitions; a new phase of community activity commenced in the 1980s when it held its hugely successful 'Fun Days'. These attracted leading stars of stage and screen, many thousands of people enjoying the entertainment. Of no less importance, through its Education Committee, Women's Guild, membership, staff and supporters, huge sums were donated each year to local charities. The Society's new Community Card fulfils the same objective and the basic Co-operative principles that were established in the middle of the 19th century are still an essential feature of trading today.

participated in the celebrations. The children's parade started from the Society's premises in Moulsham Street and marched to its meadow in Coval Lane, popularly known as the 'Co-op Field'. Many of the children that joined the parade would dress up in costumes representing products which had been manufactured by co-operatives and purchased through the Co-operative Wholesale Society. When the parade arrived at the 'Co-op Field' the cattle were chased away and everyone engaged in a variety of sporting competitions, country dancing and games. Best of all every child went home with a present of sweets, biscuits and lemonade. And for the adults there were rousing speeches from the distinguished figures within the co-operative movement.

Based on one of the historic co-operative principles - concern for the community - the Women's Guild made its own impact within Chelmsford. During the first world war, with food shortages a serious problem, the Guild played its part in ensuring that food was shared fairly. Then, when unemployment became a social catastrophe during the

Above left: International Co-operative Day, 1938 in Duke Street. **Top:** *A children's parade at an International Co-operative Day celebration in the 1930s.*

Sympathy and sincerity

Birth, marriage and death are the three great events of human condition and we would all like to think that each such occasion will be conducted with both order and dignity. Graves from the stone age show that man has always honoured his dead. The strength of feeling about death is attested to in the thousands of monuments which cover the earth. From the tombs in the Valley of Kings in Egypt to the Neolithic barrows in our own country the passing from this life has been commemorated in many ways. No-one who has spent time in a Victorian cemetery, perhaps the high water-mark in the nation's respect for the dead, can fail to be moved by the thought and care which has gone into providing lasting memorials to those who have 'gone before'.

We in the 21st century are little different, save that we are more likely to use the services of a crematorium rather than opt for an interment. We still have an immense need to properly mark the passing of those we have loved and respected during their lifetimes.

Lucking & Sons have served Chelmsford and the surrounding area since the 17th century; research has traced the family origins to the Great and Little Waltham areas of Chelmsford. In 1631 one William Lucking of Little Waltham was carrying on the trade of carpenter and joiner, and he would no doubt have been asked to make coffins. 'Undertaking' as the trade would become known has changed over the intervening years, eventually evolving to become the profession of Funeral Director, a far cry from being the side-line of the woodworking business of almost four hundred years ago.

It was however not until 1883 that William Augustus Lucking, the son of another William Lucking, bought property in New London Road, Chelmsford. These premises remain the firm's place of business, and family residence, to this day.

William Augustus had married Susan Piper of London in 1876. Their son George William Lucking, born in 1880, carried on the business following his father's death. George married Mary Hurry with whom he had two sons, Percy and Gus, and two daughters, Gladys and Doris. When George William Lucking died at the age of 41 in 1921 the business was carried on by his wife Mary until her sons came of age to succeed to the business - and in the process providing the firm's name, M Lucking & Sons.

Below: *George Lucking with his father, William Augustus, conducting a funeral of a local dignitary at Widford Church c1916.*

Only Mary Lucking's second son Gus stayed in the business, eventually taking over from his mother; he married Alice Ketley and they had two daughters, Christine and Jennifer. Christine married Bernard Gowing in 1967 and have a daughter, Sarah. Jennifer married Nicholas Mouser (Nick) in 1973 and have a son, Philip, and a daughter, Gemma. Sadly, Nick passed away in 1993. Christine and Jennifer succeeded to the business after the death of their father, Gus, in 1998. Bernard Gowing who now carries on the family business is a holder of the Diploma of Funeral Directing (Dip FD) a professional qualification requiring an examination pass set by the National Association of Funeral Directors.

In 1996 Bernard Gowing was joined by Darren Lucking grandson of Percy and great nephew of Gus Lucking.

As an independent family run business M Lucking & Sons is able to offer personal and sympathetic guidance through all the formalities of arranging the funeral of a loved one, either at Luckings' own premises or in the family home.

Luckings never closes and staff are available 24 hours a day, 365 days a year. In an age of mass production Luckings is now the only funeral directors in the area offering a large range of coffins and caskets made to exacting standards in their own workshop and made to client's individual requirements.

All funerals are carried out in a traditional and dignified manner with the option of using a horse drawn hearse or modern hearses and limousines, whilst Luckings' Masonry Department will assist clients with their choice of headstone or other memorial in addition to providing renovation and additional inscriptions to existing memorials.

In keeping with providing an evermore comprehensive service to the bereaved Luckings has also formed an association with one of the country's largest probate administration providers in order to be able to offer impartial and discrete advice covering all aspects of what to do when dealing with the deceased's affairs.

Luckings have also carried on the carpentry/joinery side of the business managed by Martin Goddard. Doors, windows and staircases are just some of the high quality products produced for many local builders.

After four hundred year or more there can surely be few firms which can match M Lucking & Sons remarkable record.

Left: *The funeral of Gus Lucking - 3rd March 1998, conducted by Bernard.*
Above left: *Gus Lucking.*
Top left: *Funeral of a local 'gentleman of the road' leaving Chelmsford Cathedral.*
Top right: *Funeral of a local police officer in the 1950s.*

The hosts with the most

In times long gone by travellers would look forward to changing horses at a coaching inn and stepping out to refresh themselves with a glass of foaming ale and perhaps warm themselves before a roaring log fire. In the 1950s and 60s however with horses becoming a distant memory the roads were already beginning to throng with cars and the transport café came into its own. Those early versions of motorway service stations were a blessing to motorists and coach travellers alike who could look forward to a warm welcome, a cup of coffee and perhaps a hamburger or an egg and bacon sandwich to sustain them on their journeys. In the intervening years many of those once well known establishments have disappeared, a few have survived almost unaltered whilst others have changed beyond all recognition.

Today the Miami Hotel and Conference Centre is a familiar sight on the A414 (A12), Princes Road, within a few minutes drive of the centre of Chelmsford. The hotel is a family owned business with three generations of the Newcombe family working together with a combined experience in the hotel and catering business of more than 150 years between them.

The hotel business traces its beginning back to 1964. Until then the site had housed Catling's Sunbeam transport café before being converted into a restaurant and later still a Wimpy Bar by the Newcombe family.

Edna and John Newcombe bought the business and premises from Catling Caterers in June 1964. They bought everything; even a dog and cat came with the business!

The Newcombes had been involved from the 1950s in the business of supplying jukeboxes and fruit machines to pubs, clubs and cafés. They had plans to build a motel and saw the potential for the restaurant belonging to Catlings, which at the time had been shut for three months.

After a cruise to Florida, the Newcombes decided to rename their new business the Miami Grill.

The Miami Grill opened in 1964. At one period the Miami extended their building to accommodate a Wimpy Drive In, which soon became the second busiest in England. Many famous names would call in at the Miami Grill: The Supremes, Stratford Johns, The Rolling Stones, Count Basie and Gene Pitney for example. All called to refresh themselves when travelling between London and Yarmouth for Sunday shows.

On building the hotel however, the Wimpy image did not fit and the franchise was ended. The hotel opened in 1971.

Below: *The original café.*
Bottom: *The café in its 'Wimpy' days.*

The new hotel originally had only two floors with a football pitch behind and the bowling green next door belonging to Crompton Parkinson. When the bowling green closed down, some of the land was bought to extend the property.

The Newcombe's children became involved in the business early on: Janice from 1964, whilst Yvonne and Colin became involved in 1970 just before the hotel opened.

Live bands and dinner dances, where one had to eat in order to drink, made the restaurant immensely popular - not least because it was the only one in Chelmsford offering such facilities.

John Newcombe passed away in 1986, but his wife, Edna has only just semi-retired.

Today, the business is run by the Newcombe's daughter Janice and grandchildren, Tony, Paula and Susan. The hotel's main customers are business reps, passing Europeans and staff from local companies such as Marconi Global Marine. Hospitality and a family atmosphere is the hotel's key to continuing success with the hotel's mission statement being simply 'satisfied customers'.

It has all come a long way from the small restaurant bought in 1964. Today, guests can enjoy A la Carte and Table d'hote menus in the Glades restaurant or bar snacks in the Retreat bar. Not surprisingly, the fifty-five bedroom luxury hotel enjoys a high occupancy rate. Meanwhile the hotel still provides accommodation for functions such as dances and weddings in public rooms, which have benefited from regular refurbishment.

Turning a restaurant into a modern hotel was no mean feat. The Miami Hotel and Conference Centre stands as a lasting tribute to John and Edna Newcombe and the commitment to putting customers first.

Above: The Wimpy Drive-in. **Top:** *An aerial view of the hotel and conference centre.* **Right:** *Left to right Martin Peters, Edna Newcombe and John Newcombe.*

Sweet success

Founded more than a hundred and forty years ago as a sugar merchanting house, today Chelmsford based James Budgett Sugars is responsible for a major share of the supply and distribution of sugar in the United Kingdom. Its long experience in sugar trading allied to its considerable know-how in accessing sugars from all sources of supply in the EU and from other countries provides a high level of expertise available to a wide range of industrial users.

An early visiting card:

> Bassett G   High St   Honiton
>
> Jan 28ᵗʰ 1929 We write Hackett as to the reason for us doing nothing with this man, he replies — I fear he is mentally unbalanced, I had to relieve him of a large bacon knife with which he was greeting people (myself in particular) since when I have not seen him.

and morning dress of the merchant trader. Staff were required to attend the office in London's Mincing Lane personally to receive their pay. The offices were Dickensian with high desks and stools with ink wells and 'dip' pens still used to write the accounts books. Warehouses and a sampling room were based beneath the offices premises.

Despite its old-fashioned image the firm however was still very much a thriving concern. David Barratt, managing director at the beginning of the new millennium, started as a junior rep with the firm in Nottingham in 1971. At that time the firm had 150 staff and had offices in all major ports and cities including Hull, Manchester and Leeds.

It was in 1857 that James Budgett first became a sugar merchant, other family members such as Samuel Budgett went into the tea trade whilst H Budgett became a cash and carry merchant selling canned goods, dried food and other provisions. Importing foodstuffs from all over the world, the Budgetts became first hand importers and agents.

The firm, James Budgett & Sons, would remain family owned and family run until 1980.

The Budgett family would became famous as race-horse owners and breeders, having three Derby winners and owning a great deal of land in Oxfordshire. The family business headquarters however remained firmly rooted in London.

The business was uncompromisingly run as a traditional London trading house. Even as late as the 1970s the Budgett family, when attending their office, still attired themselves in the black silk top hat

Sugar trading though would be turned upside down in the early 1970s. Until then the price of sugar was set each day by the world market, which was known as the 'London Daily Price'. Prices, previously governed by the sugar

Above: An early visiting card which describes a man who had to be relieved of a 'large bacon knife with which he was greeting everyone'! ***Below left:*** *Sugar sacks.*
Below: *Beacon House, home of James Budgett Sugars.*

changed its trading practices, and the reduction in the importance of London to the UK sugar market, it was decided to leave London and move to Essex, a geographical area which suited the majority of staff.

Today James Budgett sugar tankers are a familiar sight on our roads. Budgetts' bulk tanker fleet provides a round the clock delivery service within 24 hours of urgent orders being received from its many clients whilst Bextra Sugars, a subsidiary company, mills, sieves and blends special grades of refined white sugar and raw cane sugar to UK industry for groceries, drinks, baking, catering and pharmaceuticals.

merchants, then came under CAP, the Common Agricultural Policy and prices became fixed for one year. The traditional role of the sugar merchant became largely irrelevant overnight. By developing and adapting its trading practices and systems however 'JBS' evolved into the foremost sugar merchant in the industry, and by harnessing strong customer relationships the company succeeded in its new objectives and prospered.

In 1980 the Budgett family decided to leave the merchant trading business and concentrate on its farming interests in Oxfordshire. Today the company is part of the ED & F Man group of companies, itself more than 200 years old, which owns two thirds of the JBS shares. ED & F Man is one of the largest sugar and commodity trading houses in the world providing James Budgett with an intimate knowledge of the world sugar market and access to sugar sources across the globe.

James Budgett & Sons Ltd became James Budgett Sugars Ltd in August 1982.

The 1980s were marked by further integration into the sugar industry. A minority shareholding in JBS was sold to Irish Sugar, the exclusive sugar beet producer in Eire. In turn Irish Sugar is part of Greencore plc quoted on the London Stock Exchange and one of Eire's foremost food companies with expanding interests in the UK.

The move to Chelmsford took place in November 1987. Because of the way the company has

Top (both pictures): Sugar production today. **Right (both pictures):** *Lorries with James Budgett's modern-day livery.*

A continuing crusade

The Order of the Holy Sepulchre arose out of the very heart of the Crusades; it might seem difficult nowadays to feel proud of such origins. The heroics of war are often seen in a very different light today and history has revealed the base motives of so many of the crusaders, together with the horrors of cruelty and injustice inflicted on the 'infidels'. Since Vatican II, Christians have focused all their endeavours on tolerance and respect for other faiths, rather than on their destruction as tools of Satan. But the Crusades were a response to the cry 'God wills it'. Whether he did or not is beside the point. This is how the idealistic crusaders saw it.

From its establishment in 1114 AD the order of the Holy Sepulchre rapidly spread across Europe - even to the British Isles. But it is to the Low Countries that we must turn our attention to the monastery of Denkendorf in Groningen founded in 1139 AD. It is in the branch of the Order descending from this monastery that the 15th century revival took place. Back in the 12th or 13th centuries there is proof, both in Jerusalem and elsewhere of women living a 'vita religiosa' alongside canons and under the

same superior but no clear evidence of Canonesses living in autonomous communities until this 15th century revival.

At a time in English history when Catholics were suffering great persecution, and the country was undergoing the turmoil of the Civil War, Susan Hawley of Brentford, Middlesex was inspired by God to found an English Community on the continent to ensure a Catholic education for English girls. She was led to a convent of the Holy Sepulchre at Tungers in Belgium. She decided to form a community led by Mother Margaret the Novice Mistress of Tungers

Above: *The entrance to New Hall in the early 1900s.*
Left: *The front of the Palace of Beaulieu (New Hall).*
Below: *An engraving of the New Hall - 1831.*

monastery until such times as they could elect a superior of their own. Four sisters, Mother Margaret, Susan Hawley Frances Cary and a lay sister from Tungers set out for Liege and were received by a good widow woman of the town who lent them three rooms until they could be better accommodated elsewhere.

Susan Hawley was a remarkable woman and was described in the following terms 'she was large-minded and was endowed with a courage nothing could shake. Her prudence was rare and her intellect quick and penetrating, her judgment solid and enlightened'.

Christina Dennett, Prioress from 1770 to 1781, was an enlightened educationalist and a dynamic personality. Under her leadership the School flourished, 'she had her heart set on giving Catholic girls the same advantages which they would have had in the great schools in England'. In 1794, on account of the French Revolution and the disturbed situation in the Low Countries the whole Community plus the 'Pensioners' - as the girls were then called - came over to England and after a number of temporary locations finally were settled in New Hall in 1799. In 1800 a community wing was built for the nun's monastic cells and the expanding school was fitted into the main building.

In 1844 a school for the children of the neighbourhood was started and it was remarkable in that both protestants and catholics came to it. In 1879 more building was needed to accommodate increasing numbers in the school.

The community and school were evacuated during the second world war to Newnham Paddox near Rugby,

but returned to New Hall in 1946 while the restoration work was still in progress. The building had suffered bomb damage and a large part of the front of the house was demolished with considerable damage elsewhere by three bombs in 1943.

Since 1967 when the junior school was amalgamated with New Hall there has been great expansion in the building to meet increasing numbers in the school and the development of educational requirements and technology.

In the 1980s the community was inspired to embark on another venture when a Pastoral Centre was set up for the Diocese in The Barn. This serves many purposes in the fostering of prayer and spirituality. Retreats, prayer meetings conferences and workshops are held there while individuals and groups can benefit from spending a quiet time away from all the pressures of life. The Barn has a strongly ecumenical character and the project continues to develop.

Top left: *Bomb damage.*
Top right: *The 1960s building.*
Above centre: *The Arms of Henry VIII.*
Right: *New Hall today.*

So much of the city is French built

When Christopher Wren was asked what sort of memorial he would like he replied, 'Look all around you.' He was standing in St Paul's Cathedral at the time. Had the same question been posed to Frederick J French he could have put his hand on heart and said the same thing about Chelmsford. So many of the important and grand buildings in and around the city were built by the company that still bears his name. Churches, schools, pubs, bus stations and public offices all bear the French stamp of quality and taste. One of its latest ventures is the Building for the Future project at the Baptist Church on Victoria Road South. This contract is for over £1 million and is the latest in a series of building work that can be traced back to the late Victorian age.

Above left: Mr FJ French, who gave his name to the company in 1910.
Above right: An auction held in 1912.
Right: An early lorry.
Below: Chelmsford 'Omnibus Station'.

In 1895 Henry French was carrying out building work from a yard in Barrack Square. What was a little one man business has now grown into a company that has over 60 employees. Many of them have been with the company for years. They served their apprenticeships and stayed with a firm that has valued their efforts as part of a team, rather than just as members of a paid workforce. The chairman began as an apprentice

ESSEX.
CHELMSFORD
THE COUNTY TOWN.

PARTICULARS AND CONDITIONS OF SALE

"Coval Hall"
A SMALL FAMILY RESIDENCE

Three Enclosures of Fine Old Pasture Land
WITH IMMEDIATE POSSESSION

"The Red Cow"
TEMPERANCE HOTEL

Eligible Freehold Building Estate

8 acres 2 roods 21 poles

Messrs. G. B. HILLIARD & SON,

On Friday, May 17th, 1912, at 4 o'clock.

100

Chelmsford commercial scene. During the second world war the company was one of the city's main builders responding to call outs for attending to bomb damaged properties.

The company founder was not just a businessman. He had concerns for his fellow man. As a keen horticulturist he often opened his grounds to the general public. But his philanthropy went further. In his will he left the residue of his estate for the purchase of land in Broomfield Road on which homes could be built for his retired workers. Mr French would be pleased to know that, over half a century after his death, the current managing director looks as much to tradition and culture as he does to profit and expansion. It is possible to marry both sets of interests, as Frederick J French Ltd has proved. New Hall Convent and School, the 1938 Moulsham Secondary School, half a dozen churches in the third quarter of the last century and the more recent Hamilton Centre are just a handful of the examples of the impact the firm has had upon the Chelmsford skyline. It is the firm intention of all involved with Frederick J French Ltd to contribute to the provision of new landmarks that will be commented upon favourably when the 22nd century dawns.

carpenter in 1965 whilst the president joined in 1946 as an estimator and office manager. This approach by management has paid off in the loyalty shown to it. Customers have also benefited as high standards of workmanship have meant value for money. Their satisfaction has seen French's build up a valuable and consistent client base. Many have family links going back to the early part of the last century.

Frederick J French, as he always signed his letters and papers, gave his name to the company in 1910. He had worked for his father, Henry, and for Henry Potter Ltd, but set up in his own account as the Edwardian age drew to a close. In 1912 he purchased Coval Hall and its estate for £700, a princely sum nearly a century ago. The gardens included the Red Cow public house that was later to become Barclays Bank. Frederick and his wife lived at Coval Hall and ran the business from there.

After he died in 1947 the actual hall was sold, but the building company remained in the old stable yards in Cedar Avenue. The first world war broke out just two years after the hall was acquired. French employed a number of POWs who helped carry out various repair and improvement works at the Hoffmann Ball Bearing Company. This was vital war effort work. Another early contract with the giant industrial firm Marconi helped Frederick J French Ltd quickly become established as a major force in the

Above left: The Cramphorn Theatre.
Top right: New Hall - Convent of the Holy Sepulchre.
Right: New Hall School Swimming Pool.
Above right: A more modern method of transportation, part of French's new fleet.

Edmund Carr - on balance very successful

A firm of Chartered Accountants located in New London Road, Chelmsford, started in July 1953 when Kenneth Edmund Carr moved to Chelmsford to form his own business. He had recently been working for a firm of London accountants, having qualified after completing his National Service in the Navy. It was very much a family concern in the early days and his wife, Doreen helped with the administration side of things though she was a fully qualified nurse.

At that time the firm's premises were in Bank Chambers, Chelmsford and the firm was linked with a London accountancy practice called Wilson Bigg and traded as Wilson Bigg

Carr & Co from 1965 to 1970, undertaking business for local farmers and other professional clients. After seven years the firm moved to 67 New London Road but by the time another seven years had elapsed, in 1967, another move was necessary as the building was compulsorily purchased to make way for the building of Parkway. The practice remained at 13 Railway Street until January 1982 when lack of space necessitated them moving to their present address. They have recently completed the refurbishment of the ground floor and two storey accommodation at the rear of their

> *Trainee accountants who gained their experience with the firm have returned as partners*

Below: *The firm's present premises in New London Road.*

and moved to an international firm shortly afterwards, returning as partner in 1982. Ray Crace is from the Chelmsford area and qualified in 1990 with a provincial branch of an international practice, joining the company in 1999. All partners are active in the activities of the local community. Each partner brings an area of special expertise to the company, enabling the practice to offer a wide range of services including accounting, auditing, taxation advice, self assessment, payroll, information technology and financial planning. Their clients now include companies, partnerships, sole traders, regulated businesses, international subsidiaries, groups, personal taxation clients, charities and pension schemes, and offer specific expertise for doctors, dentists, and farmers.

Following the steady growth of business in Chelmsford the practice decided to open another branch in Maldon. This is run by Ray Crace and employs four people.

The partners pride themselves on giving their clients a personal service at an affordable price.

The business philosophy is that the client always comes first. Clients are well looked after and partners build up strong relationships with them. With seven partners, along with professional and secretarial support staff, all work is of the highest technical standard. Amid many other practices of varying sizes locally, Edmund Carr are one of the few which has remained independent of mergers and take-overs.

The practice intends to build on the success of the past by continuing to operate along the principles which have served them so well over the last fifty years. They will continue to seek to expand, and to remain independent. They will make use of all the benefits offered by information technology to serve their clients but there will be no change in the quality of the service they seek to give those who entrust their financial affairs to their care.

premises creating an audit room and work space for 14 people, at a cost of £250,000.

The practice has continued to grow over the years and some trainee accountants who had gained their grounding and first experience in accountancy principles and qualified with Edmund Carr later returned as partners, one such was Stewart Martin who after gaining three years experience with a prominent international firm in the City of London took up a partnership. Similarly Francis Whitbread worked for a medium sized firm in Chelmsford before returning to Edmund Carr as partner. Eric Williams came into partnership in 1991 after gaining a substantial amount of experience in Canada. Michael Vandome qualified with a medium sized London firm in 1963 and joined Edmund Carr ten years later after a period as a partner with a national firm. Malcolm Hamlyn qualified with a practice in Grays and moved to a major firm for two years after qualifying - he became a partner in 1970. David Drain trained with Edmund Carr

Above left: The firm's original premises at Bank Chambers.
Top: The current partners. Top left to right: Francis Whitbread, Ray Crace, Eric Williams, Stewart Martin. Seated left to right: David Drain, Michael Vandome, Malcolm Hamlyn.

The corner by Lloyd's Bank turning from Duke Street into Broomfield Road in a picture dating from the 1960s

Acknowledgments

Chelmsford Camera Club

Joan Brisbourne at Chelmsford Central Library

Paul Henry at Eastern Gas

Essex Chronicle Series who supplied the Royal visit photographs

Essex Libraries

CP Freeman

Thanks are also due to
John Thornton who penned the editorial text
and Steve Ainsworth for his copywriting skills